# By This You Will Know

## Streeter S. Stuart

EMETH PRESS
www.emethpress.com

*By This You Will Know*

Copyright © 2014 Streeter S. Stuart
Printed in the United States of America on acid-free paper

All rights reserved. No part of this book may be reproduced, or stored in a retrieval system or transmitted in any form or by any means, electronic, mechanical, photocopying, recording, scanning or otherwise, except as permitted by the 1976 United States Copyright Act, or with the prior written permission of Emeth Press. Requests for permission should be addressed to: Emeth Press, P. O. Box 23961, Lexington, KY 40523-3961.
http://www.emethpress.com.

Library of Congress Cataloging-in-Publication Data

Stuart, Streeter S.
 By this you will know / Streeter S. Stuart.
     pages cm
  ISBN 978-1-60947-070-8 (alk. paper)
 1. Bible--Theology. 2. Authority--Biblical teaching. 3. Power (Christian theology)--Biblical teaching. 4. Revelation--Biblical teaching I. Title.
  BS543.S78 2014
  231.7'4--dc23
                        2013050787

# Contents

## Part 1. Introduction and the New Testament

Chapter 1. Authority and Power – Divine Revelation in the Bible – Introduction / 1
Chapter 2. Beginning with Jesus – Synoptic Gospels / 7
Chapter 3. Beginning with Jesus – Gospel According to John / 13
Chapter 4. Beyond the Gospels – Acts / 19
Chapter 5. Beyond the Gospels – Romans to Revelation / 25

## Part 2. The Old Testament – Creation and God's Mighty Acts

Chapter 6. The Old Testament – Authority and Power in Creation / 33
Chapter 7. The Old Testament – Authority and Power in God's Mighty Acts – the Pentateuch / 39
Chapter 8. The Old Testament – Authority and Power in God's Mighty Acts – the Former Prophets – Joshua to 2 Kings / 51
Chapter 9. The Old Testament – Authority and Power in God's Mighty Acts – the Major Prophets / 61
Chapter 10. The Old Testament – Authority and Power in God's Mighty Acts – the Minor Prophets / 67
Chapter 11. The Old Testament – Authority and Power in God's Mighty Acts – the Writings / 73

## Part 3. Question, Response, and Conclusion

Chapter 12. Authority and Power in Question / 83
Chapter 13. The Biblical Response / 97
Chapter 14. Conclusion / 105

# Chapter 1

# Authority and Power - Divine Revelation in the Bible

## Introduction

In his book *What Jesus Demands from the World*, John Piper emphasizes the need to allow Scripture to lead us to an understanding of "what is really there." As for the Gospels and their presentation of Jesus, Piper says he realized that "there was work to be done—very hard work—to see what is really there in the God-given portrayal of Jesus in the New Testament Gospels."[1] Of the enduring value of the Gospels as they are, without academic or other re-shapings of Jesus, he says, "I will wager my life that this was God's idea and that it will be worth all my remaining breath to try to understand what is actually there and teach it faithfully."[2] Piper's concern grows from the conviction that "the church is trained to distrust the Jesus of the Gospels and to look for ever new human creations of Christ," with the result that "the real Jesus is blurred, and his power to break free from the unbiblical traditions that bind him is blunted."[3]

While the focus of this book is not the same as that of Piper's, it does share the concern . . . to show what is really there . . . especially regarding a very fundamental aspect of biblical revelation, that is, the relationship between divine authority and power. This association of authority and power permeates the Bible, and this book shows in some detail how and where authority and power are found together or in close proximity in the biblical record. From the Gospels, which are so pivotal in the presentation of Jesus, to the rest of the New Testament in its continuing presentation and defense of Jesus as the Christ and Savior, and back into the Old Testament for the unfolding revelation of the God of Abraham, Isaac, and Jacob, the two themes of authority and power are evident and compelling. Years ago a renowned German-American biblical scholar offered me this simple advice:

"Stick to the text. Stick to the text." For the most part I have done that in the basic part of this work in order to show what is really there.

The plan of the book, after this introductory chapter, is to begin with the Gospels, to continue with the rest of the New Testament, and then to go back into the Old Testament, in each case showing where and how authority and power are presented. There follows then a chapter which presents some historical reactions to the biblical presentation of divine power, especially as such power is associated with Jesus Christ, and also a chapter which attempts to show how the New Testament writers might respond to such reactions. Except where noted, the Holy Bible, New International Version (NIV) is used thought the work. Where the language is my own and not that of the NIV, I have retained the long-standing practice of capitalizing the first letters of pronouns referring to God or Jesus.

## Authority

We understand authority here to mean that certain importance, influence, right, or privilege which is recognized in a given individual, and in particular for the biblical narrative, in God and His Son Jesus Christ. Authority is closely related to power, and in some cases virtually the same, but authority is not necessarily the same as power. If, as an adult, I recognize the authority of my father or mother, it may not be because of any particular power they wield. I can respect them or recognize their authority aside from any power they may or may not have.

John Marsh has written:

> In the Bible, as in modern usage, authority is closely connected with power, though usually, but not always, distinguished from it. Its meaning covers the actual possession or use of power, the legal or moral right to exercise it, the domain (dominion) within which it is exercised, and the person or precedent appealed to in support of action or opinion. The focus of biblical usage is in the authority which belongs to God alone, all other authority being subordinate and derivative. This same divine authority was exercised by Jesus and claimed by him for the church.[4]

## Power

Power suggests a certain ability or force or even the ability to use force as needed. But power is more than suggestion. Power often involves some ability or act in or by which force is carried out or demonstrated. Edward Laarman notes that "in the [Old Testament] power and might are ascribed above all to God . . . God's power is shown both in the fact that He created the world . . . and remains more powerful than all the forces within it . . . and also in His mighty acts of salvation."[5] Thus there is a kind of two-fold focus of divine power throughout much of the biblical record. God demonstrates His power in creation and creative acts, and He also demonstrates His power in a variety of other mighty acts, many of which are referred to typically as biblical miracles. The power of God, whether in creation or other mighty acts, serves to enforce or to uphold or to demonstrate His authority.

## Basic Language

A variety of Hebrew and Greek words are translated as "authority" and "power" in the Old Testament and New Testament respectively. The focus here is not really a study of those particular words. Sometimes the words for authority or power, either in the original languages or in their translations, are present, but often authority and power are understood from the context. Suffice it to say here that the most familiar biblical words behind authority and power are the Greek words *exousia* (occurring more than 100 times in the New Testament) for authority, and *dunamis* (also occurring more than 100 times in the New Testament) for power. In the Greek translation of the Old Testament known as the Septuagint (or LXX), *exousia* is often used to translate either the Hebrew noun *memshalah*, from the verb *mashal* meaning to rule, have dominion, to reign, or variations of the Hebrew noun *shalit*, from the verb *shalat* meaning to domineer or master. Also in the Septuagint, *dunamis* is often used to translate the following: the Hebrew noun *chayil* and variations, from the verb *chul* or *chil* meaning to be firm or strong; the Hebrew noun *oz*, from the verb *azaz* meaning to be strong or mighty; and the Hebrew noun *tsabah*, from the verb *tsabah*, meaning to wage war or fight against. Thus:

| Hebrew | Greek | English |
|---|---|---|
| Memshalah | Exousia | Authority |
| Shalit | Exousia | Authority |
| Chayil | Dunamis | Power |
| Oz | Dunamis | Power |
| Tsabah | Dunamis | Power |

## Three Familiar Biblical Narratives

Here, by way of introduction, we note that this association of authority and power can be seen in three of the Bible's most familiar narratives: the struggle between David and Goliath; the survival of Shadrach, Meshach, and Abednego from the fiery furnace; and Daniel's deliverance from the lions' den. David's words to the Philistine Goliath build to the conclusion that asserts a direct relationship between the authority of God, and the power of God demonstrated in David's victory. David said in 1 Samuel 17:45, "You come against me with sword and spear and javelin, but I come against you in the name of the Lord Almighty, the God of the armies of Israel, whom you have defied." He continued in 17:46, "This day the Lord will hand you over to me . . . I'll strike you down and cut off your head . . . I will give the carcasses of the Philistine army to the birds of the air and the beasts of the earth, and THE WHOLE WORLD WILL KNOW THAT THERE IS A GOD IN ISRAEL [my caps]." David concluded in 17:47, "All those gathered here will know that it is not by sword or spear that the Lord saves; for the battle is the Lord's and he will give all of you into our hands." David's subsequent victory in the face of this formidable foe was really a victory for the *power* of God and thus affirmed the *authority* of the Lord Almighty, the God of the armies of Israel.

Shadrach, Meshach, and Abednego were condemned to the fiery furnace for failing to worship a golden image set up by King Nebuchadnezzar (see Daniel 3). They said to the king that "if we are thrown into the blazing furnace, the God we serve is able to save us from it, and he will rescue us from your hand, O king" (Daniel 3:17). When the three subsequently came out of the furnace unscathed, Nebuchadnezzar said, "Praise be to the God of Shadrach, Meshach and Abednego, who has sent his angel and rescued his servants. They . . . were willing to give up their lives rather than serve or worship any god except their own God" (Daniel 3:28). So the king decreed that "the people of any nation or language who say anything against the God of Shadrach, Meshach and Abednego be cut into pieces and their houses be turned into piles of rubble, for no other god can save in this way" (Daniel 3:29). Thus the *power* of God in delivering the three sons of Israel led to the acknowledgment of the *authority* of their God.

So it was also in the case of Daniel according to Daniel 6. Daniel was condemned for refusing to pray to any god or king other than his own God, a practice that ran counter to King Darius' own decree. The penalty for Daniel was to be thrown to the lions, but even the king said to Daniel, "May your God, whom you serve continually, rescue you!" (Daniel 6:16). When Daniel survived the ordeal, the king asked whether Daniel's God had been able to rescue him from the lions. Daniel replied, "My God sent His angel, and he shut the mouths of the lions. They have not hurt me, because I was found innocent in his sight" (6:22). The king then issued a decree (6:25-27) "that in every part of my kingdom people must fear and reverence the God of Daniel." The decree continued to exalt Daniel's God: "For he is the living God and he endures forever; his kingdom will not be destroyed, his dominion will never end. He rescues and he saves; he performs signs and wonders in the heavens and on the earth. He has rescued Daniel from the power of the lions." The *power* of God shut the mouths of the lions, and thus the *power* and *authority* of God were acknowledged even by King Darius.

## The Importance of Authority and Power

What makes a study of these two themes, authority and power, so important? The answer lies in the fact that Scripture puts them together again and again in a variety of contexts and with a variety of purposes so that one cannot be confronted by Scripture without being driven to the emphasis on divine authority and power. Ultimately, as in the case of the healing of the paralyzed man according to Mark 2:1-12 (see also Matthew 9:2-8 and Luke

5:18-26) which we will turn to in the next chapter, these two themes reveal the purpose of God in Jesus Christ and are crucial for understanding the ministry and gospel of Jesus.

People come to faith in various ways and for various particular reasons. While I lived in Ann Arbor, Michigan for a couple of years, I had a barber who was a native of the Philippines and a strong believer. When he was cutting my hair one day, we talked about how he had become a Christian. He said that the very first time he went to a church as a young man, he felt God's call on his life, and when he heard the first invitation given at that first service, he went forward to receive Christ.

It doesn't work that way for everyone. Many believers have come to faith only after considerable persuasion and reflection, and in many cases those who have come to faith did so only when they became convinced about the authority that God vested in Jesus Christ and were persuaded about the power of God working in Jesus Christ. Faith is a complex reality, and in a complex world it does not always come easily. But it does come, and it has come since the gospel was first proclaimed. Assessing and understanding the relationship between authority and power as it is revealed in Scripture may open the door of faith more readily for some people than would be the case where authority and power remain unconnected.

## The Great Commission and Authority

The Great Commission is a familiar passage found in Matthew 28:16-20:

> Then the eleven disciples went to Galilee, to the mountain where Jesus had told them to go. When they saw him they worshiped him; but some doubted. Then Jesus came to them and said, "All authority in heaven and on earth has been given to me. Therefore go and make disciples of all nations, baptizing them in the name of the Father and of the Son and of the Holy Spirit, and teaching them to obey everything I have commanded you. And surely I am with you always, to the very end of the age."

According to Matthew's Gospel, Jesus began His commission by saying, "All authority in heaven and on earth has been given to me," and He added to the commission the expectation that those who followed Him would "obey everything I have commanded you."

It is a blunt and bold assertion by Jesus, that He had been given all authority, presumably by God, in heaven and earth. And because He had been given such authority, He expected obedience to whatever He commanded. Certainly, not everyone believed then or since then that Jesus was given all authority, either by God or anyone else. He was rejected and crucified, experiencing death like death might be experienced by anyone having little or no authority. It followed and does follow that obedience to Jesus Christ and His will has never been universal. Many are not willing to be obedient to Jesus Christ, because they reject His authority.

Thus the commission must be seen for what it is, direction to those who believe what Jesus has said and who do indeed recognize His authority.

Only such people, believers, can be expected to obey whatever He commanded.

Why then do some believe and others not believe? Why have some accepted the authority of Jesus and tried to make their lives conform to His direction? And why have others not accepted the authority of Jesus and thus refused to even try to conform to His direction and teaching? One significant answer to these questions lies in how one responds to the biblical linking of authority and power. The biblical record consistently promotes a positive view of divine authority. This authority is advanced in both the Old and New Testaments. In the Old Testament, the authority of God is asserted in many passages. In the New Testament, the authority of God and Jesus is similarly asserted in many passages. To substantiate or enforce divine authority, the Bible consistently appeals to power, very often acts of power or miracles.

# Chapter 2

# Beginning with Jesus - Synoptic Gospels

The importance of the relationship between authority and power in Scripture is no more clearly evident than in the Gospels' presentation of the ministry of Jesus. One passage in particular, found in each of the Synoptic Gospels Matthew, Mark, and Luke, makes this linking of authority and power quite evident. Here we focus especially on Mark's account.

## Mark 2:1-12, Healing the Paralyzed Man

Mark 2:1-12 has parallels in Matthew 9 and Luke 5. This is the account of Jesus healing a paralyzed man. It is set in Capernaum where Jesus drew a crowd of people to a house where He spoke to them. He was in the house, but the crowd of people extended outside so that it was impossible for those who arrived late to get into the house where Jesus was speaking. Among them were four men who carried a paralyzed man, all of them apparently determined to get to Jesus to see if He could or would heal the one who was paralyzed.

What happened next has been the focus of much preaching. As a younger Christian, I remember hearing sermons on the determination and faith of the four men who brought the paralytic to Jesus. I never heard anyone speak about the real substance of the account, because I know that later in life I came to a proper understanding of the significance of this passage through my own study.

The four men apparently took their paralyzed acquaintance up to the roof of the house where Jesus was, and after making "an opening in the roof," they lowered the paralyzed man, lying on his mat, to Jesus. Jesus saw their faith, perhaps the faith of all five of them, and said to the paralytic, "Son, your sins are forgiven."

From this point, the faith of the men recedes into the background of the account. It is the evident authority of Jesus to forgive sins which comes to the forefront and which is the real point of the entire passage. Whether there were three, four or even five men who brought the paralyzed man to Jesus is the not the point. And neither is the faith of the men the real point. The account now rivets attention directly at Jesus' claim that He has forgiven the man's sins.

Considerable attention has also focused upon the fact that Jesus forgave the man's sins before he did anything else. Some have wondered why he didn't heal the man first. Others have pointed out that the spiritual problem of the man was more important than his physical condition. Such thinking also can obscure the real point of the passage.

## Focus of the Passage—Authority and Power

Some teachers of the law who were sitting in the crowd began to question themselves and perhaps each other (the Greek says literally that they were dialoging – perhaps to themselves and to one another) about the forgiveness of sin. As far as they were concerned, God alone could forgive sins, and anyone, even Jesus, who claimed to forgive sins was actually blaspheming God.

Jesus perceived what they were thinking. The passage clearly intends us to understand that even if the teachers were not dialoging with one another, Jesus was able to read their hearts and minds on the matter. When He questioned them about what they were thinking, there was no denying that He had read them correctly.

Jesus then asked the teachers two questions. First, He asked why they were thinking as they were. But He followed this question with another question: "Which is easier: to say to the paralytic, 'Your sins are forgiven,' or to say, 'Get up, take your mat and walk?'" It is this second question which is crucial for understanding the entire passage.

In a variety of church and educational settings I have asked that same question of the audiences: Is it easier to say "Your sins are forgiven," or to say, "Get up and walk"? I have often been surprised to find that many believers do not know the answer or are not sure how to respond. Perhaps those in the house at Capernaum did not know the answer as well. At Capernaum no one knew for sure that Jesus had the kind of power which could heal the paralyzed man. Part of the reason for not knowing the answer today is the very fact that much preaching and teaching on the passage fails to deal with the crux of the matter and focuses on that which recedes into the background.

What is the answer? Jesus made the answer clear. He made the answer clear by moving from the lesser to the greater logic in His explanation. The lesser or easy answer or assertion was given first: "The Son of Man has authority on earth to forgive sins." This was followed by the greater or more difficult answer or directive: "I tell you, get up, take your mat and go home." Jesus prefaced this directive by saying, "But that you may know that the Son of Man has authority on earth to forgive sins . . . ." Thus the order to take up the mat and go home was intended to substantiate the right or authority to forgive sins. And when the man picked up his mat and went home, those who were in attendance began to know or understand that maybe Jesus really did have authority to forgive sins, since He obviously had the power, evidently divine power, to bring healing to the man and enable him to go home walking. Of course in this way Jesus also said that His critics, the teachers, would know one thing by the other. They would know or recognize His authority to forgive sins by His power to heal the paralyzed man.

The account proceeds to the result of Jesus' directive to the paralyzed man: "He got up, took his mat and walked out in full view of them all." So the paralyzed man was healed, and his healing was demonstrated to all, to the critical teachers as well as to the rest of the crowd that was present. And the effect of the healing was immediate: "This amazed everyone and they praised God, saying, 'We have never seen anything like this!'" Matthew's account concludes even more pointedly in 9:8, "When the crowd saw this, they were filled with awe; and they praised God, who had given such authority to men."

## Power Validates Authority

Why was the crowd so amazed? What had the people not seen? Indeed, what had they *never* seen? They had never seen anyone healed like that. They had never seen such a demonstration of power. They may have wondered about Jesus' authority to forgive sins, but when they heard Him tell the man to get up and go home, and the man actually did so, they marveled! They realized that Jesus had special authority, because he had special power.

Here we find clearly demonstrated the relationship between authority and power. Power validates authority. Power helps to prove authority. Any claim to authority may or must be backed by power in order for such a claim to be valid. In this case, if the paralyzed man had not been able to pick up his mat and go home, the words of Jesus would have seemed foolish. The people would have laughed at Him. If He were indeed unable to heal the man, it would be assumed or evident that He also did not have authority to forgive the man's sins.

We recognize this truth for ourselves, in our own lives and circumstances. Anyone can claim the authority to forgive or pardon or absolve sins. I can do it, and you can do it. Perhaps we could go find and rent a store or other building somewhere and hang a sign out front to this effect, "Sins Forgiven; $50." Sounds kind of crazy, but it might work. At least it might work until someone came into our place of business and asked to know how we could prove that we had the authority to forgive anyone of sin. We might suggest that we were very kind and understanding practitioners of forgiveness, but our prospective customer might claim to know someone else that was kind and understanding in the dispensing of forgiveness. We might claim to be able to perform great feats of strength, but the potential customer might duplicate those feats of strength. We could stand on our heads or make other great demonstrations of physical ability. Our potential customer might do the same or know of someone who could do likewise. But if we could heal the sick, even someone who was paralyzed, we would have strong grounds on which to base our forgiving ministry.

When we drive along the highways we see signs that are there to limit speed. Usually, like most people, we notice the signs but drive faster than the posted limit. Why? Although the signs carry an authoritative warning, they are powerless. They may have been placed there at the direction of governing bodies and governing agents, but the signs have no power to enforce their message. But if we see a trooper or policeman, we respond to the authority of the sign and the trooper immediately. We do so because we know that the law enforcement official is not only an authority figure, but has the power to enforce the authority displayed in the sign. And even if we ignore the trooper, the trooper represents a power that at some point can overwhelm us and cause us to respond to the authority displayed in the sign. Power enforces authority, and without power, authority often has little meaning.

Of course, there are people who have claimed the authority to forgive sins. All they have to do is to say the words. We can say the words too. We could tell anyone that their sins are forgiven. But are they really forgiven just because we say they are forgiven? Is such forgiveness the same as forgiveness from God? How could we prove that our claim to such forgiving authority was genuine?

The authority that Jesus claimed in His forgiving the paralytic of sin was substantiated by His power to heal the man of his paralysis. The power proved the authority. The people who witnessed the healing were amazed and moved to faith.

## Elsewhere in the Synoptic Gospels

The account of the healing of the paralyzed man shows how important authority and power are for understanding the mission and message of Jesus. This passage opens our eyes to a significant aspect of the revelation that God has given us throughout the pages of Scripture. The Synoptic Gospels also demonstrate this close relationship between authority and power in several other passages.

Consider the Sermon on the Mount as an indicator of the authority of Jesus. In the Sermon on the Mount (Matthew 5-7) the authority of Jesus is clearly emphasized first in the antithetical sayings (6:21-48) which contrast the authority of the law, "You have heard that," with the authority of Jesus,

"But I tell you." This involves six specific contrasts or antithetical couplets, each of which points to the authority of Jesus.

A second clear indication of the authority of Jesus in the Sermon is found in His teaching about false prophets (7:15-23). His role in the judgment of such prophets is clear in 7:21-23: "Not everyone who says to me, 'Lord, Lord,' will enter the kingdom of heaven, but only he who does the will of my Father who is in heaven. Many will say to me on that day, 'Lord, Lord, did we not prophesy in your name, and in your name drive out demons and perform many miracles?' Then I will tell them plainly, 'I never knew you. Away from me, you evildoers.'" So Jesus asserted His authority in regard to judgment as well as eternal reward and punishment. His authority would prevail.

A third indication of the authority of Jesus in the Sermon is the emphasis placed upon His words. In 7:24 Jesus compared the wise man who built his house on the rock to "everyone who hears these words of mine and puts them into practice." In 7:26 he compared the foolish man who built his house on sand to "everyone who hears these words of mine and does not put them into practice." When the Sermon concluded, 7:28-29 indicates that the crowds who heard Jesus "were amazed at his teaching, because he taught as one who had authority, and not as their teachers of the law." So the very words of Jesus conveyed His authority.

While the Sermon on the Mount itself has no demonstration or indication of power to connect it to the clear emphasis on authority, the Sermon is followed immediately by several demonstrations of power. Matthew 8:1-4 contains the account of the healing of a man with leprosy, and begins with words that show the flow of scenes from the Sermon to the healing: "When he came down from the mountainside, large crowds followed him." The healing of the man with leprosy is followed immediately by the healing of the centurion's servant (8:5-13), and this healing is followed directly by the healing of Peter's mother-in-law (8:14-15), and by the general indication of miraculous power in 8:16: "When evening came, many who were demon-possessed were brought to him, and he drove out the spirits with a word and healed all the sick."

The demonstration of power according to Matthew 8 continues, although 8:18-22, which focuses on the cost of following Jesus, also reminds us again of the authority of Jesus as He replied to one disciple, "Follow me, and let the dead bury their own dead." Then Jesus calmed a storm (8:23-27) and healed two men who were demon-possessed (8:28-34). Again and again, by one demonstration of power after another, Jesus substantiated His divine authority. These miracles had the effect of awakening observers to the authority of Jesus. So according to 8:27, "The men were amazed and asked, 'What kind of man is this? Even the winds and the waves obey him!'" And according to 8:34, "Then the whole town went out to meet Jesus."

Throughout the Gospels of Matthew, Mark, and Luke there is considerable attention given to the authority of Jesus. But the matter of authority is not always accompanied by attention to the power which validates authority, although there are many places where the power of Jesus is demonstrated especially through His miracles.

In at least two passages, however, indications of the authority of Jesus are met by demands for signs of power. We find this in Matthew 26:57-68 as Jesus was tried by the Jerusalem Sanhedrin or Council. The authority of Jesus was questioned both in terms of His claim to destroy the temple of God and rebuild it again in three days (26:61), and in regard to whether Jesus was indeed the Messiah: "The high priest said to him, 'I charge you under oath by the living God: Tell us if you are the Christ, the Son of God'" (26:63). In 26:64 Jesus warned about the future significant demonstration of His power: "But I say to all of you: In the future you will see the Son of Man sitting at the right hand of the Mighty One and coming on the clouds of heaven." At the end of the passage, the kind of power the leaders wanted to see from Jesus is apparent as Jesus is spit upon and struck with their fists. 26:67-68 says, "Others slapped him and said, 'Prophesy to us, Christ. Who hit you?'"

In the same way, the authority of Jesus was called into question at the crucifixion according to Matthew 27:33-54. The written charge over His head said, "This is Jesus, the King of the Jews" (27:37), while some challenged Jesus to save Himself "if you are the Son of God" (27:40), and others said, "He can't save himself! He's the King of Israel!" (27:42), and still others noted that Jesus had said, "I am the Son of God" (27:43). Of course the centurion's statement was very affirming: "Surely he was the Son of God!" (27:54), and it was a recognition of authority.

These challenges to the authority of Jesus also involved requests or demands for demonstrations of power, requests which were probably not sincere. Some observers charged Jesus to "save yourself! Come down from the cross!" (27:40). Others said, "Let him come down now from the cross, and we will believe in him . . . Let God rescue him" (27:42-43), and others who thought that Jesus had called out for Elijah said, "Let's see if Elijah comes to save him" (27:49). Although such requests for demonstrations of power may not have been sincere, the requests do indicate that power was thought of as a means to substantiate the authoritative claims of Jesus.

# Chapter 3

# Beginning with Jesus - Gospel according to John

The Fourth Gospel ties together the themes of authority and power in a uniquely Johannine manner. Since John speaks of the miracles of Jesus primarily through the language of "signs," we are not surprised to find the authority of Jesus linked to the signs of Jesus. The signs that Jesus performed demonstrated His authority.

## Purpose of John's Gospel: John 20 and John 2

The purpose of John's Gospel is stated in John 20:30-31: "Jesus did many other miraculous signs in the presence of his disciples, which are not recorded in this book. But these are written that you may believe that Jesus is the Christ, the Son of God, and that by believing you may have life in his name." Here we find the authority of Jesus clearly asserted: "Jesus is the Christ, the Son of God," and believing in Him results in life. But what is the primary reason or stimulus for believing? It is the miraculous signs, some of which are recorded in John's Gospel precisely so that the readers might believe.

We can see how this relationship between authority and power works in regard to specific signs or miracles in John's Gospel. Consider the first sign, changing water into wine (John 2:1-11). The details of the account are much less important than the concluding statement in John 2:11: "This, the first of his miraculous signs, Jesus performed in Cana of Galilee. He thus revealed his glory, and his disciples put their faith in him." The power demonstrated in the sign revealed the authority of Jesus, and as a result the disciples believed in Him.

What is meant by the glory of Jesus? How does this pertain to His authority? In John 1:14 the glory of Jesus is described in this way: "The Word became flesh and made his dwelling among us. We have seen his glory, the glory of the One and Only, who came from the Father, full of grace and truth." Jesus is the Word who became flesh so that His glory was seen and understood. The glorious Jesus who came from God was full of grace and truth. Glory has to do with that which pertains to God the Father. It has to do with divine or heavenly reality. When we glorify Jesus or God, we are acknowledging or confessing that we recognize and agree that Jesus is the Son of God and that God is the Father of Jesus and that they both have a nature which is beyond this physical world.

The prayer of John 17 affirms this divine or heavenly reality in very explicit fashion. Jesus says in 17:4, "I have brought you glory on earth by completing the work you gave me to do." This means that Jesus enabled people to see and understand who God is by the very work which He Himself did. Jesus revealed God as a divine or heavenly being, His own Father. 17:5 adds, "And now, Father, glorify me in your presence with the glory I had with you before the world began." In this way Jesus testifies to His own divine or heavenly nature. His glory is that which is characterized by being in the presence of God before there was a physical realm. His glory is that He is Divine or heavenly in nature. That is what people need to see. That is the nature of His authority. And that is the source of His power. His authority is divine or heavenly, and His power is divine or heavenly as well.

The Greek word for "glory" is *doxa*. We incorporate this word in the English word "doxology." When we say or sing a doxology, we are acknowledging the heavenly nature of God or Jesus. We are recognizing God and Jesus for what they are, and we are honoring their revelation to us by believing in them.

The relationship between authority and power is seen in many other places in John's Gospel. Chapter 2 continues with John's account of Jesus driving the money changers from the temple. The response of the Jews in 2:18 was, "What miraculous sign can you show us to prove your authority to do all this?" They wanted his authority to be substantiated by signs or miracles. They wanted power to enforce authority. Jesus responded in terms of the temple being destroyed and raised again in three days, referring to His own death and resurrection, something which was not understood until after His resurrection. So 2:22 concludes, "After he was raised from the dead, his disciples recalled what he had said. Then they believed the Scripture and the words that Jesus had spoken." The power demonstrated in the resurrection led to faith in the Scripture and in Jesus Himself.

## John 3–4

In John 3, as the account of Jesus with Nicodemus begins, the words of Nicodemus to Jesus show once again the importance of power for authority. Nicodemus said in 3:2, "Rabbi, we know you are a teacher who has come from God. For no one could perform the miraculous signs you are doing if God were not with him." For Nicodemus, the signs had demonstrated the authority of Jesus.

The account of the woman at the well in John 4:1-42 also points to the relationship between authority and power. After Jesus told the woman about her private life, she drew the connection between His discerning ability and His authority, and said to others in 4:29, "Come, see a man who told me everything I ever did. Could this be the Christ?" The woman repeated her wonder at the discerning power of Jesus according to 4:39, and many of the Samaritans believed Jesus not only because of the woman's testimony but because of hearing Jesus' own words for themselves (4:41-42).

The healing of the royal official's son in 4:46-54 also shows the relationship between power and faith, with the authority of Jesus being implied by the faith of the royal official and his household. Jesus said pointedly in 4:48, "Unless you people see miraculous signs and wonders . . . you will never believe."

## John 5–7

The healing of the invalid at the pool of Bethesda, as recorded in John 5, provides another occasion for the authority of Jesus to be linked to His power. As the Jews accused Jesus of healing on the Sabbath, He said in 5:17, "My Father is always at his work to this very day, and I, too, am working." The real question of authority comes in verse 18: "For this reason the Jews tried all the harder to kill him; not only was he breaking the Sabbath, but he was even calling God his own Father, making himself equal with God." In His response, Jesus emphasized His divine authority: "For as the Father has life in himself, so he has granted the Son to have life in himself. And he has given him authority to judge because he is the Son of Man" (5:26-27).

Jesus then ties His own works (and certainly this would include His signs) to His authority as He and the Jews discuss testimonies about Jesus. In regard to the testimony of John the Baptist, Jesus says in 5:36, "I have testimony weightier than that of John. For the very work [or works, since the Greek *erga* is neuter plural] that the Father has given me to finish, and which I am doing, testifies that the Father has sent me."

In John 6, the feeding of the five thousand is another sign/miracle which results in affirmation of the authority of Jesus. So John 6:14 says, "After the people saw the miraculous sign that Jesus did, they began to say, 'Surely this is the Prophet who is to come into the world.'" But this sign did not end the quest for further demonstrations of power. When Jesus returned to the other side of the sea, He dialogued with the people about the need to believe in Himself, to recognize His authority. 6:29 says, "Jesus answered, 'The work of God is this: to believe in the one he has sent.'" And the response of the people in 6:30-31 was a request for more proof: "So they asked him, 'What miraculous sign then will you give that we may see it and believe you?  What will you do?   Our forefathers ate the manna in the desert; as it is written: "He gave them bread from heaven to eat."'"

Throughout John 6 and 7, the importance of the words of Jesus as a demonstration of His authority and as a stimulus to faith is clear.  So in 6:68 Peter said, "Lord, to whom shall we go?  You have the words of eternal life. We believe and know that you are the Holy One of God." But there is an ultimate reliance on signs or demonstrations of power to affirm His authority, as 7:31 indicates: "Still, many in the crowd put their faith in him.  They said, 'When the Christ comes, will he do more miraculous signs than this man?'"

## John 9–10

The healing of the blind man as recorded in John 9 and referred to in chapter 10 also shows the relationship between authority and power.  According to 9:3, Jesus said the healing occurred "so that the work of God might be displayed in his life." The blind man himself, after his healing, only gradually understood who Jesus was.  When he was asked who had healed him, his initial response in 9:11 was, "The man they call Jesus made some mud and put it on my eyes." Later, the Pharisees themselves were divided as to the possible divine nature of Jesus, and they questioned the man about his understanding of Jesus.  The man's response in 9:17 was, "He is a prophet."

The disputing and questioning continued according to the ongoing account of John 9.  The authority of Jesus was at the center of the dispute, and the power displayed in the healing also continued to feed the dispute.  The healed man was becoming more resolute in his assessment of Jesus, and to the objections of the Pharisees he finally asserted of Jesus in verse 33, "If this man were not from God, he could do nothing." This affirmation resulted in the man being thrown out of the synagogue, and when he had been found by Jesus, Jesus asked the man if he believed in the Son of Man (9:35).  The man asked who the Son of Man was so that he, the man, might believe in Him.  Jesus replied in 9:37, "You have now seen him; in fact, he is the one speaking with you." And verse 38 shows the conclusion of the man's progressive understanding: "Then the man said, 'Lord, I believe,' and he worshiped him."

Controversy about the nature of Jesus continues in Chapter 10 as a result of Jesus' teaching about the good shepherd, teaching which sustains the emphasis on the relationship between Jesus and His Father.  Again, the power of the sign (the healing of the blind man) surfaces in regard to the authority of Jesus.  John 10:21 indicates that some people were saying, "These are not the sayings of a man possessed by a demon.  Can a demon open the eyes of the blind?"

As chapter 10 continues, the tension between Jesus and His opponents continues.  Jesus insisted that His authority and power were from God.  He asked, according to 10:36, "Why then do you accuse me of blasphemy because I said, 'I am God's Son'?" In 10:37 He makes a direct connection to authority and power: "Do not believe me unless I do what my Father does." And in 10:38 Jesus adds emphatically: "But if I do it, even though you do not believe me, believe the miracles [works], that you may know and understand that the Father is in me, and I in the Father." Thus Jesus invites faith because of what He says, because of His words. He wants to be taken at His word. But if that is not enough, then look to the miracles or works or signs, the demonstrations of power.

## John 11–12, Lazarus

The raising of Lazarus as found in John 11 also involves the relationship between authority and power. The power displayed in the sign or miracle is obvious. Its tie to the authority of Jesus is also clear. In John 11:4, Jesus said of Lazarus, "This sickness will not end in death. No, it is for God's glory, so that God's Son may be glorified through it." Martha showed her faith in Jesus' authority. In 11:22, she said, "But I know that even now God will give you whatever you ask." And in 11:27 she said to Jesus, "Yes, Lord . . . I believe that you are the Christ, the Son of God who was to come into the world."

As the account of Lazarus draws to a close, Jesus asked Martha in John 11:40, "Did I not tell you that if you believed, you would see the glory of God?" And after the stone had been taken away at Jesus direction, He prayed to God, as 11:42 says: "I knew that you always hear me, but I said this for the benefit of the people standing here, that they may believe that you sent me." After Lazarus emerged from the tomb, 11:45 says, "Therefore many of the Jews who had come to visit Mary, and had seen what Jesus did, put their faith in him." Thus the authority of Jesus was confirmed by this act of power which led to faith in Jesus.

Chapter 12 of John's Gospel continues to play out the Lazarus sign. According to 12:9-11, a large number of Jews went to Bethany because Jesus was there and because they wanted to see Lazarus who had been raised. The tie between the authority of Jesus and the power displayed in the raising of Lazarus is indicated again in 12:10-11. The chief priests who had decided to kill Jesus (11:53) now decided to kill Lazarus also since his raising caused many to put their faith in Jesus: "So the chief priests made plans to kill Lazarus as well, for on account of him many of the Jews were going over to Jesus and putting their faith in him."

After some Greeks asked to see Jesus (12:20ff.), Jesus responded by predicting His own death. Then a strange demonstration of power also affirmed the authority of Jesus. As Jesus grimly spoke of His own death, He said in 12:28, "Father, glorify your name!" The verse continues, "Than a voice came from heaven, 'I have glorified it, and will glorify it again.'" When the crowd heard this heavenly voice, some said that it was thunder while others insisted that an angel had spoken to Jesus. But Jesus said in 12:30, "This voice was for your benefit, not mine . . . But I, when I am lifted up from the earth, will draw all men to myself."

## Two Additional Passages

Two additional passages in John's Gospel show the relationship between authority and power. As Jesus stood before Pilate, He said in 18:36,

"My kingdom is not of this world. If it were, my servants would fight to prevent my arrest by the Jews. But now my kingdom is from another place." Here Jesus asserts the potential for His power to be made known in order to substantiate and enforce His authority.

Then, in John 20, when Jesus appeared to Thomas, the evidence of His death and resurrection led to Thomas' affirmation of Jesus. Thomas said in 20:25, "Unless I see the nail marks in his hands and put my finger where the nails were, and put my hand into his side, I will not believe it." A week later Jesus did appear to Thomas, and said to him according to 20:27, "Put your finger here; see my hands. Reach out your hand and put it into my side. Stop doubting and believe." And Thomas replied in 20:28 with this affirmation of Jesus' authority: "My Lord and my God!" Jesus went on then in verse 29 to indicate that although Thomas' faith came as a result of the evidential power, it would be better to believe without seeing, without the power. But ultimately for many people, the power is necessary.

# Chapter 4

# Beyond the Gospels – Acts

## Acts 1 The Ascension of Jesus

Acts provides us with a number of passages in which the two facets of divine revelation, authority and power, are brought together. We note first the Ascension of Jesus as found in Acts 1. According to Acts 1:8, Jesus said that His followers would receive power and would become His witnesses to the ends of the earth. They would affirm His authority. He then ascended from their sight, and the two men or angels dressed in white who spoke to the people said, "This same Jesus, who has been taken from you into heaven, will come back in the same way you have seen him go into heaven" (1:11). So the Ascension of Jesus affirmed His heavenly nature and origin. It was power affirming authority.

## Acts 2 Pentecost

The Pentecost experience as found in Acts 2 also brings the authority-power connection into focus. The coming of the Holy Spirit in the Pentecost manner only confirmed the words which Jesus had previously spoken: "But wait for the gift my Father promised, which you have heard me speak about ... in a few days you will be baptized with the Holy Spirit ... you will receive power when the Holy Spirit comes on you" (Acts 1:4-8).

Peter's message on the Day of Pentecost also addressed the authority-power relationship. In 2:22, he said, "Men of Israel, listen to this: Jesus of Nazareth was a man accredited by God to you by miracles, wonders and signs, which God did among you through him, as you yourselves know." Later in the same Pentecost message, Peter spoke of the resurrection in connection with the heavenly exaltation of Jesus. Working from one of David's psalms, Peter said in 2:31 that David "spoke of the resurrection of the Christ, that he was not abandoned to the grave, nor did his body see decay."

Peter continued by noting that "God has raised this Jesus to life, and we are all witnesses of the fact. Exalted to the right hand of God, he has received from the Father the promised Holy Spirit and has poured out what you now see and hear ... God has made this Jesus whom you crucified, both Lord and Christ" (2:32-36). Thus Peter affirms that the power manifested variously in the coming of the Holy Spirit, in "miracles, wonders and signs," and in the resurrection, demonstrated the authority of Jesus as both "Lord and Christ."

## Acts 3 Healing of the Crippled Beggar

The healing of the crippled beggar as found in Acts 3 also provided for connecting the authority and power of Jesus. According to 3:6, Peter's order to the crippled man was, "In the name of Jesus Christ of Nazareth, walk." Later, according to 3:12-13, Peter denied that it was by the disciples' power that the man had been healed: "Men of Israel, why does this surprise you? Why do you stare at us as if by our own power or godliness we had made this man walk? The God of Abraham, Isaac and Jacob, the God of our fathers, has glorified his servant Jesus." Peter continued in 3:14-15, "You disowned the Holy and Righteous One ... You killed the author of life, but God raised him from the dead."

As the message progressed, Peter continued to vehemently associate the power of Jesus, evidenced in the healing of the crippled man, with His authority: "By faith in the name of Jesus, this man whom you see and know was made strong. It is Jesus' name and the faith that comes through him that has given this complete healing to him, as you can all see" (3:16). Peter left no uncertainty about the nature of Jesus and the source of His power. The prophets had foretold the suffering of God's Christ (3:17-18), and it was incumbent on the people to repent "so that your sins may be wiped out, that times of refreshing may come from the Lord, and that he may send the Christ, who has been appointed for you—even Jesus" (3:19-20). Jesus was now in heaven "until the time comes for God to restore everything" (3:21), but He was the one prophesied by Moses who said, "The Lord your God will raise up for you a prophet like me from among your own people; you must listen to everything he tells you. Anyone who does not listen to him will be completely cut off from among his people" (3:22-23). Indeed, all the prophets and the covenants anticipated the coming of Jesus, through whom all the peoples of the earth would be blessed, although "God sent him first to you to bless you by turning each of you from your wicked ways" (3:24-26).

## Acts 4 Affirmation and Arrest

Later, according to Acts 4, when Peter and John were arrested and taken before the Sanhedrin, Peter again found opportunity to connect the power displayed in the healing of the crippled man, and in the resurrection of Jesus, to the authority of Jesus. He said in 4:9-10, "If we are being called to account today for an act of kindness shown to a cripple and are asked how he was healed, then know this, you and all the people of Israel: It is by the name of Jesus Christ of Nazareth, whom you crucified but whom God raised from the dead, that this man stands before you healed." Peter added in 4:12, "Salvation is found in no one else, for there is no other name under heaven given to men by whom we must be saved." When Peter and John had been released and met with other followers of Jesus, they prayed that the power of God would be manifest through the authority of Jesus: "Now, Lord, consider their threats and enable your servants to speak your word with great boldness. Stretch out your hand to heal and perform miraculous signs and wonders through the name of your holy servant Jesus" (4:29-30).

## Acts 5 Peter Speaks to the Sanhedrin

Before the Sanhedrin again, Peter's speech in Acts 5:27-32 includes this affirmation in 5:30-31: "The God of our fathers raised Jesus from the dead – whom you had killed by hanging him on a tree. God exalted him to his own right hand as Prince and Savior, that he might give repentance and forgiveness of sins to Israel." The power displayed in the resurrection is thus tied to Jesus' authority in His exaltation as Prince and Savior.

## Acts 7 Stephen

Acts 7 records Stephen's speech before his martyrdom. In reviewing Israel's history Stephen touched on a number of evidences of divine power such as the "wonders and miraculous signs" performed in Egypt through Moses (7:36). He eventually spoke of the prophets who were persecuted and who "predicted the coming of the Righteous One" (7:52). As he was being stoned, Stephen affirmed the authority of Jesus as we learn from 7:55-56: "But Stephen, full of the Holy Spirit, looked up to heaven and saw the glory of God, and Jesus standing at the right hand of God. 'Look,' he said, 'I see heaven open and the Son of Man standing at the right hand of God.'"

## Acts 9 Paul's Personal Experience of Power

Paul's blinding, powerful vision and conversion on the road to Damascus precipitated his affirmation and preaching of the authority of Jesus. After going to the house of Ananias where his eyesight was restored, he went to Damascus where he spent several days with disciples. Acts 9:20 says, "At once he began to preach in the synagogues that Jesus is the Son of God." Then 9:22 adds, "Yet Saul grew more and more powerful and baffled the Jews living in Damascus by proving that Jesus is the Christ." This experience of Paul which brought him directly to the relationship between the power and authority of Jesus is reiterated elsewhere in Acts, even as the personal testimony of Paul. Various miracles or demonstrations of power which were performed by Peter or Paul according to Acts thus served as important stimuli for leading people to recognize the divine authority in Jesus and to become believers in Him.

## Acts 10 Peter's Preaching

The preaching done by Peter and Paul also brought together the emphasis on the authority and power of Jesus. In Acts 10, Peter's message at the house of Cornelius mentioned "how God anointed Jesus of Nazareth with the Holy Spirit and power, and how he went around doing good and healing all who were under the power of the devil, because God was with him" (10:38). Continuing, Peter said in 10:40-43, "God raised him from the dead on the third day and caused him to be seen . . . he is he one whom God appointed as judge of the living and the dead. All the prophets testify about him that everyone who believes in him receives forgiveness of sins through his name."

## Acts 13 Paul's Preaching

When Paul delivered his first missionary message in Antioch of Pisidia, according to Acts 13, he noted of Jesus that "God raised him from the dead, never to decay" (13:34), and reiterated in 13:37, "The one whom God raised from the dead did not see decay." This power demonstrated in Jesus affirmed his authority. So 13:38-39 declares: "I want you to know that through Jesus the forgiveness of sins is proclaimed to you. Through him everyone who believes is justified from everything you could not be justified from by the law of Moses."

## Acts 16 Paul and the Philippian Jailer

The account of the Philippian jailer in Acts 16 also shows how a demonstration of power or miracle reinforced the message of the authority of Jesus. The jailer was so affected by the miraculous release of Paul and Silas that he asked what he needed to do to be saved. The response was "Believe in the Lord Jesus, and you will be saved—you and your household" (16:31). The resulting joy of the jailer, as noted in 16:34, occurred "because he had come to believe in God – he and his whole family."

## Acts 17 Paul at Thessalonica and Athens

Here we note that while in Thessalonica, Paul reasoned with the Jews (Acts 17) in the synagogue. The focal points of his reasoning are found succinctly in 17:3: power, "explaining and proving that the Christ had to suffer and rise from the dead;" and authority, "This Jesus I am proclaiming to you is the Christ." In Athens it was the same: authority, "He has set a day when he will judge the world with justice by the man he has appointed;" and power, "He has given proof of this to all men by raising him from the dead" (17:31).

## Acts 28 Paul on Malta

Finally, we may simply observe that according to Acts 28:1-6, when Paul and others were shipwrecked on the island of Malta during his trip to Rome, Paul was bitten by a viper which he shook off into a fire "and suffered no ill effects." This unusual demonstration of power led the people who saw it to change their opinion about Paul being a murderer, and to suggest that "he was a god," an unusual conferring of authority.

# Chapter 5

# Beyond the Gospels — Romans to Revelation

The rest of the New Testament also shows the connection between authority and power that has already been seen in the Gospels and Acts. From the writings of Paul to the Apocalypse or Revelation, power is seen as that which authenticates authority. The focus is clearly upon Jesus, that the power of God displayed in and through Him affirmed His authority as the Son of God, the Christ or Messiah, and the Lord of life and salvation.

## Romans

In Romans we may note the following passages which speak of the relationship between authority and power. With respect to the gospel of God, Paul wrote in Romans 1:3 "regarding his Son, who as to his human nature was a descendant of David, and who through the Spirit of holiness was declared with power to be the Son of God by his resurrection from the dead: Jesus Christ our Lord." Then in Romans 6, as Paul explained the meaning and significance of baptism, he related the power of the resurrection to the new life found in submission to the authority of Christ: "Just as Christ was raised from the dead through the glory of the Father, we too may have a new life" (6:4); and "if we have been united with him like this in his death, we will certainly also be united with him in his resurrection" (6:5). So 6:9-10 adds, "For we know that since Christ was raised from the dead, he cannot die again . . . the life he lives, he lives to God."

Power and authority are also evident in Romans 8:34 which says, "Christ Jesus, who died—more than that, who was raised to life—is at the right hand of God and is also interceding for us." Romans 14:9 also asserts, "For this very reason, Christ died and returned to life so that he might be the Lord of both the dead and the living." And in Romans 15:17-19 Paul speaks of the divine authority which has been understood through his ministry: "Therefore I glory in Christ Jesus in my service to God. I will not venture to speak of anything except what Christ has accomplished through me in leading the Gentiles to obey God." This has happened by power, "by what I have said and done—by the power of signs and miracles through the power of the Spirit."

## 1 Corinthians

The obvious and impressive association of authority and power in 1 Corinthians comes in chapter 15, the great resurrection chapter of the Bible. But first we may note 1 Corinthians 6:14 which says, "By his power God raised the Lord from the dead, and he will raise us also." The power of God is evident not only in the resurrection of Jesus, but also in repentant sinners being raised to a new life of faith, and in their ultimate resurrection to heavenly life. The authority of Christ is shown in Christ being raised *first*, and as 6:15 says, in the fact that the bodies of believers become members of Christ himself, or as 6:17 asserts, "But he who united himself with the Lord is one with him in spirit."

1 Corinthians 15 repeatedly affirms the bodily resurrection of Jesus: 15:4 says that "he was raised on the third day according to the Scriptures," while 15:20 continues, "Christ has indeed been raised from the dead, the first fruits of those who have fallen asleep." By this power, the authority of Christ is affirmed as in 15:22, "For as in Adam all die, so in Christ all will be made alive. But each in his own turn: Christ, the firstfruits; then, when he comes, those who belong to him." Then according to 15:24-25, "he hands over the kingdom to God the Father after he has destroyed all dominion, authority and power. For he must reign until he has put all his enemies under his feet." And Paul is clear in 15:27-28 that God will put everything but Himself under Christ, and that everything else has been put under Christ. Thus victory over sin and death is ultimately attributable "to God! He gives us the victory through our Lord Jesus Christ" (15:57).

## 2 Corinthians

Two passages are significant for our purposes in 2 Corinthians. First, there is 5:11-21 which emphasizes the reconciliation with God that believers find in Christ. 5:15 mentions Christ "who died for them and was raised again." This note of power is followed significantly by the familiar words of authority in 5:17: "Therefore, if anyone is in Christ, he is a new creation; the old has gone, the new has come!" And the passage continues: "All this is from God, who reconciled us to himself through Christ and gave us the ministry of reconciliation: that God was reconciling the world to himself in

Christ" (5:18-19). The conclusion in 5:21 is, "God made him who had no sin to be sin for us, so that in him we might become the righteousness of God."

Then there is 2 Corinthians 13:3-4 where Paul directed his attention to those who raised the question of authority by "demanding proof that Christ is speaking through me." His response was very basic: "For to be sure, he was crucified in weakness, yet he lives by God's power. Likewise, we are weak in him, yet by God's power we will live with him to serve you."

## Galatians

Galatians opens by combining authority and power in its address: "Paul, an apostle — sent not from men nor by man, but by Jesus Christ and God the Father, who raised him from the dead" (1:1). The word of authority continues in the benediction that follows: "Grace and peace to you from God our Father and the Lord Jesus Christ, who gave himself for our sins to rescue us from the present evil age, according to the will of our God and Father, to whom be glory for ever and ever. Amen" (1:3-5).

## Ephesians

Ephesians also begins by emphasizing the authority of Jesus Christ and basing His authority on the power of God demonstrated in Him. Chapter 1 is full of the message of authority beginning especially with the Blessing/Thanksgiving that opens in 1:3-4: "Praise be to the God and Father of our Lord Jesus Christ, who has blessed us in the heavenly realms with every spiritual blessing in Christ. For he chose us in him before the creation of the world." The chapter continues to the power that works in believers, the same power that raised Christ from the dead: "That power is like the working of his mighty strength, which he exerted in Christ when he raised him from the dead and seated him at his right hand in the heavenly realms" (1:19-20). The mark of authority then continues, culminating in 1:22: "And God placed all things under his feet and appointed him to be head over everything for the church, which is his body, the fullness of him who fills everything in every way."

## Philippians

The authority that is inherent in Jesus is found in a number of places in Philippians. We may note especially how 2:9 says that "God exalted him to the highest place and gave him the name that is above every name." Then 3:20-21 adds that "our citizenship is in heaven. And we eagerly await a Savior from there, the Lord Jesus Christ, who, by the power that enables him to bring everything under his control, will transform our lowly bodies so that they will be like his glorious body." In this context, Paul also directs the reader to the power of Jesus Christ and writes in 3:10 of his desire to "know Christ and the power of His resurrection."

## Colossians

The Letter to the Colossians mixes the power and authority of Jesus Christ in significant fashion, especially throughout 1:15-23. Here the power is especially seen in the creative role of Christ and in His resurrection. 1:15-16 says, "He is the image of the invisible God, the firstborn over all creation. For by him all things were created: things in heaven and on earth, visible and invisible, whether thrones or powers or rulers or authorities; all things were created by him and for him." The passage continues to say in 1:18, that "he is the head of the body, the church; he is the beginning and the firstborn from among the dead, so that in everything he might have the supremacy."

Chapter 2 also brings the power and authority of Christ into focus. According to 2:9, "in Christ all the fullness of the Deity lives in bodily form," and continuing, God "disarmed the powers and authorities [and] made a public spectacle of them, triumphing over them by the cross" (2:15). We participate in His power by baptism, as 2:12 says, "having been buried with him in baptism and raised with him through your faith in the power of God, who raised him from the dead." And 3:1 almost summarizes such power and authority: "Since, then, you have been raised with Christ, set your hearts on things above, where Christ is seated at the right hand of God."

## 1 Thessalonians

In 1 Thessalonians we find power demonstrated by the resurrection of Jesus. 4:14 says, "We believe that Jesus died and rose again and so we believe that God will bring with Jesus those who have fallen asleep in him." The authority of Jesus surfaces in a number of passages, but in close association with the assertion of power. So in 4:16 "the Lord himself will come down from heaven, with a loud command, with the voice of the archangel and with the trumpet call of God." Later 5:9 asserts, "For God did not appoint us to suffer wrath but to receive salvation through our Lord Jesus Christ."

## Hebrews

This work, which has been described variously as a letter or homily, exalts Jesus and thus asserts His authority at many places, especially through a number of comparisons. Jesus is the Son of God and thus higher than the angels. He is more significant than Moses. His priesthood is better than any earthly priesthood. His ministry is more significant than any previous ministry because He is the minister of a better covenant than the preceding covenant. And His sacrifice is better than any other sacrifice, and was a once for all sacrifice. In this way Hebrews leaves no doubt about the authority of Jesus.

So what of the power? Hebrew 2 describes the salvation which has come through Jesus. 2:3-4 says, "This salvation, which was first announced by the Lord, was confirmed to us by those who heard him. God also testified to it by signs, wonders and various miracles, and gifts of the Holy Spirit distributed according to his will." And in 5:7-8 we find this somewhat oblique reference to power, perhaps to both the resurrection and Ascension: "During the days of Jesus' life on earth, he offered up prayers and petitions with loud cries and tears to the one who could save him from death, and he was heard because of his reverent submission . . . he learned obedience from what he suffered and, once made perfect, he became the source of eternal salvation for all who obey him and was designated by God to be high priest in the order of Melchizedek."

## 1 Peter

1 Peter's opening blessing or praise begins with this word of authority and power:

> "Praise be to the God and Father of our Lord Jesus Christ! In his great mercy he has given us new birth into a living hope through the resurrection of Jesus Christ from the dead, and into an inheritance that can never perish, spoil or fade—kept in heaven for you, who through faith are shielded by God's power until the coming of the salvation that is ready to be revealed in the last time."

The authority and power are also evident in chapter 3. Thus 3:18 says, "For Christ died for sins once for all, the righteous for the unrighteous, to bring you to God. He was put to death in the body but made alive by the Spirit." And the passage continues to speak of baptism that "saves you by the resurrection of Jesus Christ, who has gone into heaven and is at God's right hand—with angels, authorities and powers in submission to him."

## 2 Peter

The authority of Jesus comes immediately to the fore in 2 Peter where 1:2 exalts "the righteousness of our God and Savior Jesus Christ." This perspective on authority continues through the first chapter to 1:11 which says that "you will receive a rich welcome into the eternal kingdom of our Lord and Savior Jesus Christ."

The emphasis on authority is supported by a significant word of power centering on the transfiguration of Jesus. So 1:16 says, "We did not follow cleverly invented stories when we told you about the power and coming of our Lord Jesus Christ, but we were eyewitnesses of his majesty." The passage continues with a sense of both authority and power: "For he received honor and glory from God the Father when the voice came to him from the Majestic Glory, saying, 'This is my Son, whom I love; with him I am well pleased.' We ourselves heard this voice that came from heaven when we were with him on the sacred mountain" (1:17-18). Such power enforces prophetic authority as 1:19 says: "And we have the word of the prophets made more certain, and you will do well to pay attention to it."

Subsequently, the message is reinforced by three examples of power. First is the fact that "God did not spare angels when they sinned, but sent them to hell, putting them into gloomy dungeons to be held for judgment" (2:4). Then there is the example of Noah who was protected by God even though He, God, "did not spare the ancient world," but "brought the flood on its ungodly people: (2:5). And third, there is the example of Lot who was rescued by God who "condemned the cities of Sodom and Gomorrah by burning them to ashes, and made them an example of what is going to happen to the ungodly" (2:6). 2:9-10 concludes by warning that God will bring punishment to "those who follow the corrupt desire of the sinful nature and despise authority."

## Jude

The authority of Jesus is shown clearly in this small letter. Verse 4 speaks of those who "deny Jesus Christ our only Sovereign and Lord." The doxology in verses 24-25 offers "glory, majesty, power and authority" to "the only God our Savior . . . through Jesus Christ our Lord, before all ages, now and forevermore! Amen."

The power that is appealed to is found in a number of historical examples: the deliverance from Egypt, as in verse 5, "the Lord delivered his people out of Egypt, but later destroyed those who did not believe"; and the examples of Sodom and Gomorrah, as in verse 7, which with "the surrounding towns gave themselves up to sexual immorality and perversion. They serve as an example of those who suffer the punishment of eternal fire." Divine power is also evident in the fall of angels (verse 6), the death of Moses (verses 8-9), and the examples of Cain, Balaam, and Korah (verse 11).

## Revelation

The authority of God the Father, and Jesus Christ the Son, is prominent throughout Revelation. It is after all, "the revelation of Jesus Christ which God gave him to show his servants" (1:1). From that opening, to the close which says in 22:16, "I, Jesus, have sent my angel to give you this testimony for the churches. I am the Root and the Offspring of David, and the bright Morning Star," we never lose sight of divine authority. Notably, chapters 4 and 5 picture the throne of heaven, where praise is continuous and absolute: "Holy, holy, holy is the Lord God Almighty, who was, and is, and is to come" (4:8); and "Worthy is the Lamb, who was slain, to receive power and wealth and wisdom and strength and honor and glory and praise" (5:12).

The power that supports the authority in Revelation is seen in a number of ways. First, there is the revelation itself which God gave to Jesus, who "made it known by sending his angel to his servant John, who testifies to everything he saw—that is, the word of God and the testimony of Jesus

Christ" (1:1-2). The revelation is accompanied by the closing warning, that "if anyone adds anything to them [the words of the prophecy of this book], God will add to him the plagues described in this book," and "will take away from him his share in the tree of life and in the holy city, which are described in this book" (22:18-19).

Second, there is the personal power (although perhaps it is better described as authority) of John himself. Certainly there is sufficient justification/evidence to contend that John the Apostle is the writer. He says in 1:9 that he was a "brother and companion in the suffering and kingdom and patient endurance that are ours in Jesus."

Then there are the clear indications of the resurrection of Jesus as found in such passages as 1:5 which mentions "Jesus Christ, who is the faithful witness, the firstborn from the dead," or 1:17-18 where one like a son of man says, "I am the First and the Last. I am the Living One; I was dead, and behold I am alive for ever and ever! And I hold the keys of death and Hades."

Fourth, there are references to the evidence of creation and to the creative power of God and His Son. For instance, 4:11 says, "You are worthy, our Lord, and God, to receive glory and honor and power, for you created all things, and by your will they were created and have their being." And 10:5-6 mentions the angel who raised his hand to heaven and "swore by him who lives for ever and ever, who created the heavens and all that is in them, the earth and all that is in it, and the sea and all that is in it."

Finally there is the sheer power of the scope of the revelation. It reveals an understanding of God who controls not only the physical world, but the flow of human history.

# Chapter 6

# The Old Testament — Authority and Power in Creation

The Old Testament gives birth to the New Testament in many ways. We should not be surprised to find that the Old Testament presents the same kind of association of authority and power that is found in the New Testament. The historical situation may change, and the characters involved may differ, but there is nothing different about the God who is revealed in the Old Testament. He is the God of creation, the God of Abraham and Moses, the God of the prophets, and the God of the coming Messiah whom the New Testament reveals as Jesus the Messiah or Christ. God is the ultimate authority above all persons and things, and He has demonstrated or supported His authority by His powerful acts again and again.

The authority of God is asserted frequently in the Old Testament. The power that enforces or demonstrates God's authority is also operative or present in many Old Testament passages. This power is of two basic types: power demonstrated in God's creation and His creative activity, and power demonstrated in God's mighty acts beyond creation. We turn first to those Old Testament passages which show a rather close connection between God's authority and His creative power. These particular Old Testament passages do not exhaust the passages which point to the creative power of God.

## Genesis

Genesis 1:1 begins with an assumptive assertion of God's authority, "In the beginning God," and continues with an ultimate statement of God's power, "[God] created the heavens and the earth." The account of creation reaches its apex in the creation of humanity: "God created man in his own image, in the image of God he created him; male and female he created them" (1:27). 2:1 speaks succinctly about the extent of the creation: "Thus the heavens and the earth were completed in all their vast array."

The subsequent account of the temptation and fall of Adam and Eve (Genesis 3) leaves no doubt about the authority of God who warns that disobedience to His command will bring punishment, but shows that God's authority is subject to rejection. Thus the punishing power of God is displayed in death itself (3:3), in the earthly travail of humanity with the pain of childbirth and the toil of work (3:15-17), and in the expulsion from the Garden of Eden (3:23-24).

## 1 Chronicles

1 Chronicles 16:7-36 records David's psalm of thanksgiving. This psalm speaks significantly of the authority of God in respect to His creative power. So 16:23-25 says, "Sing to the Lord, all the earth; proclaim his salvation day after day. Declare his glory among the nations, his marvelous deeds among all peoples. For great is the Lord and most worthy of praise; he is to be feared above all gods." This recognition of the Lord's authority continues in verses 28-30: "Ascribe to the Lord . . . glory and strength, ascribe to the Lord the glory due his name . . . worship the Lord in the splendor of his holiness," etc. The power which affirms the Lord's authority is seen in verses 26-27: "For all the gods of the nations are idols, but the Lord made the heavens. Splendor and majesty are before him; strength and joy in his dwelling place."

## Job

Job also addresses the combined emphasis on authority and power as displayed in creation. Chapter 38 is perhaps the best example as God speaks to Job from the storm or whirlwind and asks, "Where were you when I laid the earth's foundation?" (38:4), and "Who shut up the sea behind doors when it burst forth from the womb . . . when I said, 'This far you may come and no farther?'" (38:8-11). The conversation between Job and God continues in this vein through chapter 42 as the authority of God is also acknowledged, first by God: "Will the one who contends with the Almighty correct him? Let him who accuses God answer him!" (40:2); and then by Job: "I know that you can do all things; no plan of yours can be thwarted" (42:2).

## Psalms

The authority and power of God as asserted and evidenced through creation surface at many other points in the Old Testament, and certainly in the book of Psalms as can be seen in the psalms that we refer to here.

Psalm 8 begins and ends (8:1,9) with praise for God's authority: "O Lord, our Lord, how majestic is your name in all the earth!" The power of God as displayed in nature supports this authority: "You have set your glory above the heavens . . . your heavens, the work of your fingers, the moon and the stars which you have set in place" (8:1-3). And the power is demonstrated in humanity: "What is man that you are mindful of him, the son of man that you care for him? You made him a little lower than the heavenly beings and crowned him with glory and honor. You made him ruler over the works of your hands; you put everything under his feet" (8:4-6).

Psalm 19 exudes the authority of God, and this psalm combines the authority and power of God in its first verse: "The heavens declare the glory of God; the skies proclaim the work of his hands." Psalm 29:1-2 recognizes the authority of God in much the same way as 1 Chronicles 16:28-29 : "Ascribe to the Lord, O mighty ones, ascribe to the Lord glory and strength. Ascribe to the Lord the glory due his name; worship the Lord in the splendor of his holiness." Then 29:3-11 recognizes God's creative power in the storm: "The voice of the Lord is over the waters; the God of glory thunders, the Lord thunders over the mighty waters . . . The voice of the Lord strikes with flashes of lightning . . . The Lord sits enthroned over the flood; the Lord is enthroned as King forever . . . ."

Psalm 89 speaks of the authority of the Lord, first in terms of His great love (verses 1 and 2), then in terms of His faithfulness (also verses 1 and 2), and thirdly in terms of the blessings of the covenant through the lineage of David [perhaps the Messiah] (verses 3-4). This authority is backed by the testimony of power: "The heavens praise your wonders, O Lord...For who in the skies above can compare with the Lord?" (verses 5-6). The psalm continues: "You rule over the surging sea; when its waves mount up, you still them . . . The heavens are yours, and yours also the earth; you founded the world and all that is in it . You created the north and the south . . . Your arm is endued with power; your hand is strong, your right hand exalted" (verses 9-13). Psalm 95 succinctly combines recognition of the authority and power of God. So 95:1 says, "Come, let us sing for joy to the Lord; let us shout aloud to the Rock of our salvation," and 95:3 says, "For the Lord is the great God, the great King above all gods," while verses 6-7 add, "Come, let us bow down in worship, let us kneel before the Lord . . . for he is our God." 95:5 then speaks of God's power: "The sea is his, for he made it, and his hands formed the dry land;" and 95:6 says that we kneel before the Lord "our Maker."

We can also see the combination of authority and power in Psalms 119 and 121. Indication of the authority of God is found throughout Psalm 119, but note especially 119:89, "Your word, O Lord, is eternal; it stands firm in the heavens," and 119:91, "Your laws endure to this day, for all things serve you." Between these affirmations of the authority of God, the psalmist says, "You established the earth, and it endures" (119:90). In Psalm 121 the authority of God is expressed in terms of His help (121:1-2): "My help comes from the Lord," and His power follows accordingly since the Lord is "the Maker of heaven and earth" (121:2).

# Prophetic Literature

## Isaiah

The prophets also reveal in many passages the relationship between authority and power. This is especially true of Isaiah. Perhaps no one verse in Isaiah captures the sense of authority more succinctly than 33:22: "For the Lord is our judge, the Lord is our lawgiver, the Lord is our king; it is he who will save us."

Isaiah includes many notable examples of the relationship between authority and the power of creation. Consider Isaiah 40 in which authority and power are intertwined. So 40:22 says, "He sits enthroned above the circle of the earth . . . He stretches out the heavens like a canopy, and spreads them out like a tent to live in." In 40:25 the Holy One of Israel asks, "To whom will you compare me? Or who is my equal?" Then verse 26 responds, "Lift your eyes and look to the heavens: Who created all these? He who brings out the starry host one by one, and calls them each by name. Because of his great power and mighty strength, not one of them is missing."

Isaiah's Servant passages also demonstrate the closeness between authority and creative power. So Isaiah 42:1 says of the Servant's authority, "Here is my servant, whom I uphold, my chosen one in whom I delight; I will put my Spirit on him and he will bring justice to the nations." And 42: 8 adds, "I am the Lord; that is my name! I will not give my glory to another or my praise to idols." Then in this context, 42:5 speaks of creative power: "This is what God the Lord says—he who created the heavens and stretched them out, who spread out the earth and all that comes out of it, who gives breath to its people, and life to those who walk on it."

Consider also Isaiah 44. Here the authority of God is expressed in verse 6 as one of many assertions of authority: "This is what the Lord says—Israel's King and Redeemer, the Lord Almighty; I am the first and I am the last; apart from me there is no God." And what of the power that confirms such authority? It is affirmed in 44:24: "I am the Lord who has made all things, who alone stretched out the heavens, who spread out the earth by myself."

Isaiah 45 declares the authority of God again and again in terms such as those found in 45:5: "I am the Lord, and there is no other; apart from me there is no God." The creative power of God follows as in 45:7: "I form the light and create darkness, I bring prosperity and create disaster; I, the Lord, do all these things." 45:12 adds, "It is I who made the earth and created mankind upon it. My own hands stretched out the heavens; I marshaled their starry hosts."

The juxtaposition of authority and power is seen again in 51:12-16. In verse 12 the Lord says, "I even I, am he who comforts you," and in verse 13, He wonders why His people "forget the Lord your Maker, who stretched out the heavens and laid the foundations of the earth." He states in 51:15-16, "For I am the Lord your God, who churns up the sea so that its waves roar—the Lord Almighty is his name . . . I who set the heavens in place, who laid the foundations of the earth, and who say to Zion, 'You are my people.'"

Finally for Isaiah, we note the connection between authority and power in chapters 65-66. Chapter 65 begins with these words: "I revealed myself to those who did not ask for me; I was found by those who did not seek me." Then in 65:11-12 the Lord says, "But as for you who forsake the Lord and forget my holy mountain . . . I will destine you for the sword, and you will bend down for the slaughter; for I called but you did not answer, I spoke but you did not listen. You did evil in my sight and chose what displeases me." Such authority is also affirmed in 66:4: "So I also will choose harsh treatment for them and will bring upon them what they dread. For when I called, no one answered, when I spoke no one listened. They did evil in my sight and chose what displeases me."

As for the association with creation in this particular context, we note 65:17-18: "Behold, I will create new heavens and a new earth. The former things will not be remembered, nor will they come to mind. But be glad and rejoice forever in what I will create, for I will create Jerusalem to be a delight and its people a joy." Then according to 66:1-2 the Lord says, "Heaven is my throne and the earth is my footstool . . . Has not my hand made all these things, and so they came into being?" And in 66:22 the Lord says that "the new heavens and the new earth that I make will endure before me."

## Jeremiah

The association of authority and creative power is also found in several places in Jeremiah. Jeremiah 10:10, for instance, speaks of the Lord's authority: "But the Lord is the true God; he is the living God, the eternal King. When he is angry, the earth trembles; the nations cannot endure his wrath." There follow in 10:11-16 words of the Lord's creative power, beginning with, "Tell them this: 'These gods, who did not make the heavens and the earth, will perish from the earth and from under the heavens.' But God made the earth by his power; he founded the world by his wisdom and stretched out the heavens by his understanding," and concluding with, "He who is the Portion of Jacob . . . is the Maker of all things, including Israel, the tribe of his inheritance—the Lord Almighty is his name."

Jeremiah 31 also associates the authority of God with His creative power. 31:31-34 records Jeremiah's prophesy of a new covenant between God and Israel. God's authority is clear (italics are mine): "*I* will make a new covenant . . . It will not be like the covenant *I* made with their forefathers when *I* took them by the hand to lead them out of Egypt . . . they broke *my* covenant . . . This is the covenant *I* will make with the house of Israel . . . *I* will put *my* law in their minds . . . *I* will be their God and they will be *my* people . . . they will all know *me* . . . *I* will forgive their wickedness and will remember their sins no more."

There follows in 31:35-37 a passage which emphasizes creative power: "This is what the Lord says, he who appoints the sun to shine by day, who decrees the moon and stars to shine by night, who stirs up the sea so that its waves roar—the Lord Almighty is his name: Only if these decrees vanish from my sight . . . will the descendants of Israel ever cease to be a nation before me . . . Only if the heavens above can be measured and the foundations of the earth below be searched out will I reject all the descendants of Israel."

Jeremiah 51 also associates divine authority and creative power. In 51:1, the Lord says, "See, I will stir up the spirit of a destroyer against Babylon . . . I will send foreigners to Babylon to winnow her and to devastate her land," and 51:5 asserts, "For Israel and Judah have not been forsaken by their God, the Lord Almighty, though their land is full of guilt before the Holy One of Israel." Then creation comes to the fore in 51:15: "He made the earth by his power; he founded the world by his wisdom and stretched out the heavens by his understanding." 51:16 continues, "When he thunders, the waters in the heavens roar; he makes clouds rise from the ends of the earth. He sends lightning with the rain and brings out the wind from his storehouses." And 51:19 echoes 10:16 as previously noted: "He who is the Portion of Jacob . . . is the Maker of all things, including the tribe of his inheritance—the Lord Almighty is his name."

## Amos

Among the Minor Prophets, Amos and Zechariah speak briefly to the relationship between the Lord's authority and His creative power. Amos 4:13 says: "He who forms the mountains, creates the wind, and reveals his thoughts to man, he who turns dawn to darkness, and treads the high places of the earth—the Lord God Almighty is his name."

## Zechariah

Zechariah 12 is notable for its association of God's authority and creative power. Assertions of the Lord's authority permeate Zechariah's work, and in chapter 12 we note especially that it is "the word of the Lord" (12:1) which is directed towards Judah and Jerusalem "because the Lord Almighty is their God" (12:5). And reference to God's creative power is found also in 12:1 which says that it is the Lord "who stretches out the heavens, who lays the foundation of the earth, and who forms the spirit of man within him."

# Chapter 7

# The Old Testament —Authority and Power in God's Mighty Acts

We have seen how the Old Testament associates the authority of God with His creative power. There are many other passages in the Old Testament which direct the attention of the reader to the twin themes of authority and power, particularly in regard to what may be called the power demonstrated or inherent in God's mighty acts. These acts are basically of two kinds, those that deal with nature, and those that deal with human life and the course of human events. In the latter case, it is especially evident in the prophets that God's power is demonstrated in the course of national events, including events that occur in or affect pagan nations or occur in or affect Israel itself.

## The Pentateuch

### Genesis

We can look to the flood account in Genesis 6-9 as an example. The authority of God is scattered throughout the passage. Consider 6: 3, "Then the Lord said, 'My Spirit will not contend with man forever, for he is mortal'"; and 6:6-7, "The Lord was grieved that he had made man on the earth, and his heart was filled with pain. So the Lord said, 'I will wipe mankind, whom I have created, from the face of the earth . . . for I am grieved that I have made them.'" The flood itself is a significant example of power in an act of punishment and salvation which supports the authority of God. So in Genesis 6:13 God said to Noah, "I am going to put an end to all people, for the earth is filled with violence because of them. I am surely going to destroy both them and the earth." And in the aftermath of the flood, God said, "Never again will I curse the ground because of man, even though every inclination of his heart is evil from childhood. And never again will I destroy all living creatures, as I have done" ((8:21). According to Genesis 9, God established a covenant with Noah and his sons which involved formation of the rainbow as a powerful sign of the covenant: "I have set my rainbow in the clouds, and it will be the sign of the covenant between me and the earth. Whenever I bring clouds over the earth and the rainbow appears in the clouds, I will remember my covenant between me and you and all living creatures of every kind" (9:13-15).

God's dealings with Abraham also evidence the relationship between authority and power. The authority is seen in the initial call of Abraham according to Genesis 12:1-3 in which the Lord said that He would make a great nation of Abraham and would bless him, and in Genesis 17:1-2 according to which the Lord appeared to Abraham and said, "I am God Almighty; walk before me and be blameless. I will confirm my covenant between me and you and will greatly increase your numbers."

The power of God is demonstrated in the case of Abraham in several ways including the miraculous birth of a child to Sarah in her old age, and the destruction of the cities of Sodom and Gomorrah. So far as the miraculous birth of Isaac is concerned, Genesis 17:16 says that God spoke to Abraham concerning Sarah and said, "I will bless her and will surely give you a son by her. I will bless her so that she will be the mother of nations; kings of peoples will come from her." Abraham's response was to fall facedown and laugh with incredulity. But God said to him in 17:19–21, "Yes, but your wife Sarah will bear you a son, and you will call him Isaac. I will establish my covenant with him as an everlasting covenant for his descendants after him ... But my covenant I will establish with Isaac, whom Sarah will bear to you by this time next year." Sarah laughed too when she heard the news (18:10-12), and the Lord's response to Abraham was quite direct: "Why did Sarah laugh and say, 'Will I really have a child, now that I am old?' Is anything too hard for the Lord? I will return to you at the appointed time next year and Sarah will have a son" (18:13-14).

The destruction of Sodom and Gomorrah also showed the connection between authority and power. The angel who talked with Abraham about the impending destruction is called "God" or "the Lord" as in the account of the birth announcement (so 18:17, 19, 20, 22, 26, 27, 30, 31, 32, 33; see also 19:14, 16, 24, and 27). The destruction is clearly regarded as the work of God: "The Lord is about to destroy the city" (19:14); "Then the Lord rained down burning sulfur on Sodom and Gomorrah—from the Lord out of the heavens. Thus he overthrew those cities and the entire plain, including all those living in the cities" (19:24-25); "So when God destroyed the cities of the plain, he remembered Abraham, and he brought Lot out of the catastrophe that overthrew the cities where Lot had lived" (19:29).

## Exodus

There are a number of examples from the life of Moses which show the connection between authority and power. The call of Moses at the burning bush is one (Exodus 3). The power of God was evident in the bush that was not consumed: "Moses saw that though the bush was on fire it did not burn up" (3:2). When Moses investigated, God asserted His authority: "I am the God of your father, the God of Abraham, the God of Isaac and the God of Jacob" (3:6). When Moses later asked about the name of God that he should convey to the Israelites, God replied to him, ""I AM WHO I AM. This is what you are to say to the Israelites: 'I AM has sent me to you'" (3:14). And God said again, "Say to the Israelites, 'The Lord, the God of your fathers—the God of Abraham, the God of Isaac and the God of Jacob—has sent me to you.' This is my name forever, the name by which I am to be remembered from generation to generation" (3:15).

With the power of the burning bush experience behind him, and the Lord's authority made expressly clear, Moses experienced a second demonstration of power and renewed indication of authority. He was told by God that he must go to Egypt to lead the Hebrews out of Egypt to the desert and then to the "land flowing with milk and honey" (3:17). But God also told Moses that the king of Egypt would resist attempts to free the Israelites, so that God would have to "stretch out my hand and strike the Egyptians with all the wonders that I will perform among them" (3:20). Anticipating a confrontation with the Egyptians, and perhaps the Hebrew people, Moses asked what he should do if his word was not believed and the Lord's revelation was rejected. Moses was told to throw his staff on the ground, and when he did "it became a snake, and he ran from it" (4:3). Then Moses was told to pick the snake up by the tail, and so "he reached out and took hold of the snake and it turned back into a staff in his hand" (4:4). This demonstration of the Lord's power was followed by an assertion of authority: "This ... is so that they may believe that the Lord, the God of their fathers—the God of Abraham, the God of Isaac and the God of Jacob—has appeared to you" (4:5).

There was another demonstration of power in support of authority, and indication that even more demonstrations of power might be necessary. According to 4:6-7, Moses was told to put his hand into his cloak, so that "when he took it out, it was leprous, like snow." Then Moses was told to put his hand back into his cloak so that "when he took it out, it was restored, like the rest of his flesh." The Lord said to Moses in 4:8-9, "If they do not believe you or pay attention to the first miraculous sign, they may believe the second. But if they do not believe these two signs or listen to you, take some water from the Nile and pour it on the dry ground. The water you take from the river will become blood on the ground." Thus there was need for demonstrations of power to validate the authority of God which was being exercised through Moses.

This attention to authority and power is rather constant in the subsequent events that took Moses back to Egypt and led to the formal exodus of the Israelites from Egypt. So 4:28 says that "Moses told Aaron everything the Lord had sent him to say, and also about all the miraculous signs he had commanded him to perform." Moses and Aaron then reported to the Israelites what had happened, as 4:29 says: "Aaron told them everything the Lord had said to Moses. He also performed the signs before the people and they believed. And when they heard that the Lord was concerned about them and had seen their misery, they bowed down and worshiped."

The actual challenge to God's authority that precipitated the plagues in Egypt comes at the beginning of Exodus 5. Here Moses and Aaron said to Pharaoh in 5:1, "This is what the Lord, the God of Israel, says: 'Let my people go, so that they may hold a festival to me in the desert.'" Pharaoh's reply to Moses and Aaron was a challenge to the authority of God: "Who is the Lord, that I should obey him and let Israel go? I do not know the Lord and I will not let Israel go" (5:2).

In subsequent chapters, the emphasis on the authority of God as well as His power is woven throughout the narrative of Israel's deliverance. In Exodus 6:6-8, the Lord said to Moses, "I am the Lord, and I will bring you out from under the yoke of the Egyptians . . . I will redeem you with an outstretched arm and with mighty acts of judgment. I will take you as my own people, and I will be your God. Then you will know that I am the Lord your God . . . I am the Lord."

It is clear from the Exodus narrative that the authority of God was extended to Moses and Aaron, and that the power exhibited through them was a sign of God's power substantiating both God's and their authority. According to Exodus 7:1, the Lord said to Moses, "See, I have made you like God to Pharaoh, and your brother Aaron will be your prophet." Then in 7:3-5 God spoke of His power: "Though I multiply my miraculous signs and wonders in Egypt, he [Pharaoh] will not listen to you. Then I will lay my hand on Egypt and with mighty acts of judgment I will bring out my divisions, my people the Israelites. And the Egyptians will know that I am the Lord when I stretch out my hand against Egypt and bring the Israelites out of it."

The series of miracles or signs before Pharaoh began with the staff of Moses becoming a snake (Exodus 7:8-13) and swallowing up the staffs of the Egyptian magicians. Then the ten plagues brought the authority of God directly into focus, with the power of God displayed in the plagues. The first plague, involving the waters of the Nile being changed to blood (Exodus 7:14-24), showed this clearly. In 7:16 Moses was instructed to say to Pharaoh, "The Lord, the God of the Hebrews, has sent me to say to you: Let my people go, so that they may worship me in the desert." Then 7:17 adds, "This is what the Lord says: By this you will know that I am the Lord: With the staff that is in my hand I will strike the water of the Nile, and it will be changed into blood." Thus the authority of God was to be demonstrated and substantiated by the power of the plague. The plagues continued to the death of the firstborn and occupy much of what follows in Exodus 7-12. The emphasis on authority and power is perhaps epitomized by the introduction to the plague of locusts in 10:1-2. Here the Lord said to Moses, "Go to Pharaoh, for I have hardened his heart and the hearts of his officials so that I may perform these miraculous signs of mine among them that you may tell your children and grandchildren how I dealt harshly with the Egyptians and how I performed my signs among them, and that you may know that I am the Lord." The future commemoration of the Passover would always be a reminder of God's authority and power as Moses informed the Israelites: "In days to come, when your son asks you, 'What does this mean?' say to him, 'With a mighty hand the Lord brought us out of Egypt, out of the land of slavery . . . This is why I sacrifice to the Lord . . . And it will be like a sign on your hand and a symbol on your forehead that the Lord brought us out of Egypt with his mighty hand'" (13:14-16).

The actual crossing of the sea together with the destruction of the Egyptians in their pursuit of the Israelites also provided opportunity for the authority and power of God to be demonstrated. According to Exodus 14:4, the Lord said to Moses, ""I will harden Pharaoh's heart, and he will pursue them. But I will gain glory for myself through Pharaoh and all his army, and the Egyptians will know that I am the Lord." When the Israelites balked at continuing their journey, Moses responded with the famous words of 14:13-14: "Do not be afraid. Stand firm and you will see the deliverance the Lord will bring you today. The Egyptians you see today you will never see again. The Lord will fight for you; you need only to be still." Then Moses was told to raise his staff over the waters which would divide so that the Israelites could cross the sea on dry ground. 14:17 reiterates: "I will harden the hearts of the Egyptians so that they will go in after them. And I will gain glory through Pharaoh and all his army, through his chariots and his horsemen. The Egyptians will know that I am the Lord when I gain glory through Pharaoh, his chariots and his horsemen." The crossing of the sea and the destruction of the Egyptians had its intended effect. Accordingly 14:31 says, "When the Israelites saw the great power the Lord displayed against the Egyptians, the people feared the Lord and put their trust in him and in Moses his servant."

The song of Moses and Miriam which follows in Exodus 15 also lauds the Lord's authority and power. 15:6-8 says, "Your right hand, O Lord, was majestic in power. Your right hand, O Lord, shattered the enemy. In the greatness of your majesty you threw down those who opposed you . . . By the blast of your nostrils the water piled up." 15:11-12 adds, "Who among the gods is like you, O Lord? Who is like you—majestic in holiness, awesome in glory, working wonders? You stretched out your right hand and the earth swallowed them." As the song continues to mention the enemies ahead in Canaan and the conquest of the land, 15:16 says, "By the power of your arm they [enemies] will be as still as a stone," and 15:18 exalts the Lord: "The Lord will reign for ever and ever." Finally, in one renowned sentence, Miriam acknowledged the authority and power of the Lord: "Sing to the Lord for he is highly exalted. The horse and its rider he has hurled into the sea" (15:21).

Subsequent to these particular events associated with leaving Egypt, the concern for authority and power surfaces in many passages in the rest of the book of Exodus. Here we note only a few such passages.

When Jethro, the father-in-law of Moses, learned that Israel was passing through the Sinai region, he went with his family to meet Moses. After Jethro heard details of the turn of events in Egypt, he praised God by acknowledging the power manifested for Israel's deliverance and by exalting the Lord's authority. He said, "Praise be to the Lord, who rescued you from the hand of the Egyptians and of Pharaoh, and who rescued the people from the hand of the Egyptians. Now I know that the Lord is greater than all other gods, for he did this to those who had treated Israel arrogantly" (Exodus 18:10-11).

The divine manifestations on Sinai in connection with the giving of the commandments brought together the power and authority of God. Exodus 20:18 says, "When the people saw the thunder and lightning and heard the trumpet and saw the mountain in smoke, they trembled with fear." So the people said to Moses in 20:19, "Speak to us yourself and we will listen. But do not have God speak to us or we will die." Moses responded, "Do not be afraid. God has come to test you, so that the fear of God will be with you to keep you from sinning" (20:20). Nevertheless, "the people remained at a distance" (20:21), and the Lord said to Moses, "Tell the Israelites this: 'You have seen for yourselves that I have spoken to you from heaven; Do not make any god to be alongside me; do not make for yourselves gods of silver or gods of gold'" (20:22-23).

## Leviticus

The institution of sacrifice as recorded in Leviticus 9-10 also provided an opportunity for the authority and power of God to be demonstrated in the life of Israel. According to Leviticus 9:22-24, after Moses and Aaron came out of the Tent of Meeting, "They blessed the people; and the glory of the Lord appeared to all the people." Then, "Fire came out from the presence of the Lord and consumed the burnt offering and the fat portions on the altar. And when all the people saw it, they shouted for joy and fell facedown." There follows immediately in Leviticus 10 the account of the death of Nadab and Abihu. The independent actions of these two sons of Aaron defied the authority of the Lord: "And they offered unauthorized fire before the Lord, contrary to his command" (10:1). The power of the Lord was evident in punishment: "So fire came out from the presence of the Lord and consumed them, and they died before the Lord. Moses then said to Aaron, 'This is what the Lord spoke of when he said: "Among those who approach me I will show myself holy; in the sight of all the people I will be honored"'" (10:2-3).

Later Leviticus 26 associates the Lord's power in punishment with the failure of Israel to respond positively to His authority. 26:14-15 warns about what will happen "if you will not listen to me and carry out all these commands, and if you reject my decrees and abhor my laws and fail to carry out all my commands and so violate my covenant." The punishment is a demonstration of God's power: "I will bring upon you sudden terror, wasting diseases and fever that will destroy your sight and drain away your life. You will plant seed in vain, because your enemies will eat it. I will set my face against you so that you will be defeated by your enemies . . . I will punish you for your sins seven times over" (26:16-18).

## Numbers

Punishment thus became a significant tool in God's attempt to gain respect for His authority, and there are a number of instances where power in punishment surfaces for this purpose according to Numbers. Here we may consider Numbers 11 in which a food problem surfaces again. Exodus 16 contains the first account of the Lord's providing manna and quail for the Israelites. Both accounts are opportunities for demonstrating the power of God in support of His authority. The miraculous provisions of food speak for themselves so far as power is concerned. As for authority, in Exodus 16:6-7 Moses and Aaron said, "In the evening you will know that it was the Lord who brought you out of Egypt, and in the morning you will see the glory of the Lord, because he has heard your grumbling against him." Then Moses added in 16:8, "You will know that it was the Lord when he gives you meat to eat in the evening and all the bread you want in the morning, because he has heard your grumbling against him. Who are we? You are not grumbling against us, but against the Lord."

The account of the manna and quail in Numbers 11 also served to bolster the authority of the Lord. It began with God's fiery response to the complaining of the people (11:1-3), and went on to the desire of the people for food, especially meat, like they had in Egypt. The provision of quail was not only a provision but a kind of punishment. According to 11:23, the Lord said to Moses, "Is the Lord's arm too short? You will now see whether or not what I say will come true for you." The Lord not only provided quail, but after the quail had been gathered, "the anger of the Lord burned against the people, and he struck them with a severe plague" (11:31-33).

Respect for the authority of the Lord and for His prophet Moses was also something Aaron and Miriam needed to learn. Although they were Moses' brother and sister, Numbers 12 shows that they had a certain jealousy of Moses' role as God's spokesman, and asked, "Has the Lord spoken only through Moses? . . . Hasn't he also spoken through us?" (12:2). The result was that Miriam was afflicted with leprosy. Aaron then acknowledged to Moses their lack of respect: "Please, my lord, do not hold against us the sin we have so foolishly committed" (12:11). Moses then interceded on behalf of Miriam who was confined outside the camp for seven days before she was allowed to return to the people so that the Israelites could resume their journey (12:13-15).

The reaction of the Israelites to the report of the spies who searched out the land of Canaan (Numbers 13-14) also produced one of Israel's most serious challenges to the Lord's authority as well as a significant demonstration of the Lord's power. The Lord's authority was especially challenged in regard to the leadership of Moses: "All the Israelites grumbled against Moses and Aaron . . . And they said to each other, 'We should choose a leader and go back to Egypt'" (Numbers 14:2-4). Even Joshua could not persuade the people to relent: "Only do not rebel against the Lord. And do not be afraid of the people of the land . . . Their protection is gone, but the Lord is with us" (14:9).

When the Israelites wanted to stone Moses, Aaron, Joshua, and Caleb, the Lord's response to Moses showed the concern for authority and power. He said in 14:11, "How long will these people treat me with contempt? How long will they refuse to believe in me, in spite of all the miraculous signs I have performed among them?" Even though the Lord relented from His expressed intention to destroy the Israelites, He indicated that He would demonstrate His authority by the punishment that would be inflicted on Israel. He said in 14:21-23, "Nevertheless, as surely as I live and as surely as the glory of the Lord fills the whole earth, not one of the men who saw my glory and the miraculous signs I performed in Egypt and in the desert but who disobeyed me and tested me ten times—not one of them will ever see the land I promised on oath to their forefathers. No one who has treated me with contempt will ever see it."

Two additional accounts in Numbers of God's punishment of Israel also show the relationship between authority and power. The first concerns the rebellion under the leadership of Korah, Dathan, and Abiram (Numbers 16). When these three leaders and their principal followers opposed the leadership of Moses and Aaron, they opposed the very authority of God. They said, "You have gone too far! The whole community is holy, every one of them, and the Lord is with them. Why then do you set yourselves above the Lord's assembly?" (16:3). Moses responded, "In the morning the Lord will show who belongs to him and who is holy . . .The man the Lord chooses will be the one who is holy. You Levites have gone too far!" (16:5-7). Moses emphasized the fact that the Lord had given Korah, Dathan, and Abiram with their sons a significant ministry, but by trying to gain the priesthood they were opposing God's will and authority. He said, "It is against the Lord that you and all your followers have banded together. Who is Aaron that you should grumble against him?" (16:8-11).

The rebellion persisted, and when the time came that the Lord was about to punish the rebels, Moses said that the power of God would be evident in the manner of the punishment, that it would not be through natural death but through a cataclysmic opening of the earth to swallow up those who were to be punished. By this, he said, "you will know that these men have treated the Lord with contempt" (16:30). 16:31 indicates that such a cataclysm did indeed take place, that "the earth opened its mouth and swallowed them, with their households and all Korah's men and all their possessions." Additionally, 250 men who were offering incense were incinerated by fire (16:35), and the metal from their censers was used to overlay the altar according to the direction of the Lord and with the warning that "no one except a descendant of Aaron should come to burn incense before the Lord, or he would become like Korah and his followers" (16:40). And when rebellion continued, 14,700 people died as a result of a punishing plague (16:46-50).

In conjunction with this particular challenge to God's authority as well as that of His servants, Moses and Aaron, the budding of Aaron's staff (Numbers 17) also served to draw attention to the divinely ordered authority for ministering at the tabernacle/Tent of Testimony. Moses took the staffs of Aaron and the leaders of the twelve tribes into the Tent of Testimony, and when he retrieved them the next day, only Aaron's staff had sprouted and grown buds as witnessed by the leaders. The Lord said to Moses, "This will put an end to their grumbling against me, so that they will not die" (17:10), although the Israelites said to Moses, "We will die! We are lost, we are all lost!" (17:12). But in Numbers 18 the Lord made it very clear that no Israelite would die if the Lord's directions for ministering at the Tent were followed correctly.

A second additional account of punishment which brought the authority and power of God into focus had to do with the bronze snake/serpent as found in Numbers 21:4-9. As Israel progressed on its journey and bypassed Edom, according to 21:5, "they spoke against God and against Moses, and said, 'Why have you brought us up out of Egypt to die in the desert? There is no bread! There is no water! And we detest this miserable food.'" Then the Lord punished the people with venomous snakes/serpents so that the people cried for relief: "We sinned when we spoke against the Lord and against you. Pray that the Lord will take the snakes away from us" (21:7). In response to Moses' prayer the Lord directed Moses to erect a bronze snake on a pole so that "when anyone was bitten by a snake and looked at the bronze snake, he lived" Through this demonstration of power the people learned respect for the Lord's authority.

## Deuteronomy

Deuteronomy contains a number of passages that bring together the authority of God as associated with His power. Several of these are noted here. The opening chapters of Deuteronomy anticipate the entrance of the Israelites into Canaan. Toward the end of chapter 3, Moses emphasized the authority and power of God as he spoke of his own punishment at being refused entry into the land: "O Sovereign Lord, you have begun to show to your servant your greatness and your strong hand. For what god is there in heaven or on earth who can do the deeds and mighty works you do?" (3:24).

In chapter 4 Moses commanded the people to be obedient upon their entrance to the land and to avoid idolatry and all its trappings. In 4:32 he said, "Ask now about the former days, long before your time, from the day God created man on the earth; ask from one end of the heavens to the other. Has anything so great as this ever happened, or has anything like it ever been heard of?" What was the great thing that had happened? Moses answered accordingly in 4:34, "Has any god ever tried to take for himself one nation out of another nation, by testings, by miraculous signs and wonders, by war, by a mighty hand and an outstretched arm, or by great and awesome deeds, like all the things the Lord your God did for you in Egypt before your very eyes?"

Moses continued this line of thought in 4:35 as he emphasized the authority of God: "You were shown these things so that you might know that the Lord is God; besides him there is no other." Then he returned to speaking of the power of God in 4:36-38: "From heaven he made you hear his voice to discipline you. On earth he showed you his great fire, and you heard his words from out of the fire . . . he brought you out of Egypt by his Presence and his great strength, to drive out before you nations greater and stronger than you and to bring you into their land and to give it to you for your inheritance." Then again he urged respect for God's authority: "Acknowledge and take to heart this day that the Lord is God in heaven and on the earth below. There is no other" (4:39).

As Moses continued his review of God's dealings with Israel, he urged the people to remember for their posterity the power which God had demonstrated as a means of reinforcing the Lord's authority. Moses said, according to Deuteronomy 6:20, that in the future when Israelite sons asked, "What is the meaning of the stipulations, decrees and laws the Lord our God has commanded you?" they were to respond, "We were slaves of Pharaoh in Egypt, but the Lord brought us out of Egypt with a mighty hand" (6:21). And he continued, "Before our eyes the Lord sent miraculous signs and wonders—great and terrible—upon Egypt and Pharaoh and his whole household. But he brought us out from there to bring us in and give us the land that he promised on oath to our forefathers" (6:22-23). And he again emphasized the authority of the Lord: "The Lord commanded us to obey all these decrees and to fear the Lord our God, so that we might always prosper and be kept alive, as is the case today. And if we are careful to obey all this law before the Lord our God, as he has commanded us, that will be our righteousness" (6:24-25).

Deuteronomy 8 continues Moses' review of God's dealings with Israel during the course of the Exodus period. Very succinctly Moses connected the power of God with the authority of God in 8:10-20. 8:11 says, "Be careful that you do not forget the Lord your God, failing to observe his commands, his laws and his decrees that I am giving you this day." And he continued to warn in 8:14 that with settlement in the land and personal success, "your heart will become proud and you will forget the Lord your God, who brought you out of Egypt, out of the land of slavery." According to

8:16, Moses spoke of God's power: "He gave you manna to eat in the desert, something your fathers had never known, to humble and to test you so that in the end it might go well with you." So there was to be no question of authority: "You may say to yourself, 'My power and the strength of my hands have produced this wealth for me.' But remember the Lord your God, for it is he who gives you the ability to produce wealth, and so confirms his covenant, which he swore to your forefathers, as it is today" (8:17-18).

Noteworthy too is Deuteronomy 11 in which the mountains Gerizim and Ebal are designated as mountains of blessing and cursing. The chapter begins with a charge from Moses to maintain respect for the authority of the Lord: "Love the Lord your God, and keep his requirements, his decrees, his laws and his commands always" (11:1). Then Moses reviewed briefly the powerful acts of God: "Remember . . . his majesty, his mighty hand, his outstretched arm; the signs he performed and the things he did in the heart of Egypt, both to Pharaoh king of Egypt and to his whole country; what he did to the Egyptian army, to its horses and chariots, how he overwhelmed them with the waters of the Red sea . . . how the Lord brought lasting ruin on them" (11:2-4). He continued to remind them of "what he did to Dathan and Abiram, sons of Eliab the Reubenite, when the earth opened its mouth . . . and swallowed them up with their households," and that "it was your own eyes that saw all these great things the Lord has done" (11:6-7).

Chapters 27 and 28 of Deuteronomy bring the curses and blessings associated with the mountains Ebal and Gerizim into focus again. In 28:15 Moses said, "However, if you do not obey the Lord your God and do not carefully follow all his commands and decrees I am giving you today, all these curses will come upon you and overtake you," and he goes on to list and explain the curses, and to show that the curses themselves will become a demonstration of God's power for future generations. So 28:45-48 says, "All these curses will come upon you. They will pursue you and overtake you until you are destroyed, because you did not obey the Lord your God and observe the commands and decrees he gave you. They will be a sign and wonder to you and your descendants forever . . . you will serve the enemies the Lord sends against you. He will put an iron yoke on your neck until he has destroyed you."

From this point on, both Deuteronomy and the larger Old Testament place increased emphasis on the importance of the power of God as seen in Israel's defeat and punishment to indicate the nation's lack of respect for the authority of God. Deuteronomy 29 shows this clearly in the context of the renewing of the covenant in the land of Moab. According to 29:2-8, Moses began his address to the people with a review of the powerful acts that brought Israel to the threshold of Canaan. He said, "Your eyes have seen all that the Lord did in Egypt to Pharoah, to all his officials and to all his land. With your own eyes you saw those great trials, those miraculous signs and great wonders." Then the Lord spoke: "During the forty years that I led you through the desert, your clothes did not wear out, nor did the sandals on your feet. You ate no bread and drank no wine or other fermented drink. I did this so that you might know that I am the Lord your God."

Emphasis on respect for God's authority into future generations continues through the recitation of the covenant, and this leads to the recognition that when Israel is not faithful to God, His power will be seen in Israel's defeat and destruction. So 29:22-24 says, "Your children who follow you in later generations and foreigners who come from distant lands will see the calamities that have fallen on the land and the diseases with which the Lord has afflicted it . . . All the nations will ask: 'Why has the Lord done this to this land? Why this fierce, burning anger?'" The answer follows in 29:25: "It is because this people abandoned the covenant of the Lord, the God of their fathers . . . They went off and worshipped other gods and bowed down to them, gods they did not know, gods he had not given them . . . Therefore the Lord's anger burned against this land . . . the Lord uprooted them from their land, and thrust them into another land."

Finally we note how the Song of Moses in Deuteronomy 32 also combines the themes of authority and power. Thus 32:3 says of God's authority, "I will proclaim the name of the Lord. Oh, praise the greatness of our God! He is the Rock, his works are perfect, and all his ways are just. A faithful God who does no wrong, upright and just is he." Then 32:23-24, among a near litany of punishments, warns of God's punishing power unleashed against faithless Israel: "I will heap calamities upon them and spend my arrows against them. I will send wasting famine against them, consuming pestilence and deadly plague." And 32:36-39 says clearly, "The Lord will judge his people and have compassion on his servants . . . He will say: 'Now where are their gods, the rock they took refuge in . . . See now that I myself am He! There is no god besides me. I put to death and I bring to life, I have wounded and I will heal, and no one can deliver out of my hand.'"

# Chapter 8

# The Old Testament —Authority and Power in God's Mighty Acts

## The Former Prophets—Joshua to 2 Kings

### Joshua

In Joshua we see the authority and power of God evidenced in the encounter with the prostitute Rahab prior to Israel's conquering and destruction of Jericho. When Israel's two spies reached Jericho and met with Rahab, she left no uncertainty about her people's respect for the authority of the Lord. According to Joshua 2:9, she said, "I know that the Lord has given this land to you and that a great fear of you has fallen on us, so that all who live in this country are melting in fear because of you." And she added, "When we heard of it, our hearts melted and everyone's courage failed because of the you, for the Lord your God is God in heaven above and on the earth below" (2:11). What was it that they had heard and that motivated this respect for the Lord's authority? They had heard of God's powerful acts: "We have heard how the Lord dried up the water of the Red Sea for you when you came out of Egypt, and what you did to Sihon and Og, the two kings of the Amorites east of the Jordan, whom you completely destroyed" (2:10).

The crossing of the Jordan River also provided opportunity for the authority and power of God to be addressed. In 4:21-23, Joshua said to the people, "In the future when your descendants ask their fathers, 'What do these stones mean?' tell them, 'Israel crossed the Jordan on dry ground.' For the Lord your God dried up the Jordan before you until you had crossed over. The Lord your God did to the Jordan just what he had done to the Red Sea when he dried it up before us until we had crossed over." This demonstration of the Lord's power pointed to His authority: "He did this so that all the people of the earth might know that the hand of the Lord is powerful and so that you might always fear the Lord your God" (4:24).

Finally in Joshua, we see the emphasis on authority and power in the covenant renewal that took place at Shechem according to Joshua 24. Here Joshua reviewed the history of God's dealing with Israel, beginning with Abraham and working down to the crossing of the Jordan and the conquering of the land of promise. In the familiar words of 24:14-15 Joshua encouraged faithfulness to the Lord's authority: "Now fear the Lord and serve him with all faithfulness. Throw away the gods your forefathers worshiped beyond the River and in Egypt, and serve the Lord . . . But as for me and my household, we will serve the Lord." The people responded affirmatively in 24:16-18: "Far be it from us to forsake the Lord to serve other gods . . . We too will serve the Lord, because he is our God." And the reason for the affirmation was the demonstrated power: "It was the Lord our God himself who brought us and our fathers up out of Egypt, from that land of slavery, and performed those great signs before our eyes. He protected us on our entire journey and among all the nations . . . And the Lord drove out before us all the nations . . . who lived in the land" (24:17-18).

## Judges

The Book of Judges shows clearly how the authority of God can be forgotten or ignored when the power of God is neglected or forgotten. According to Judges 2:7, "The people served the Lord throughout the lifetime of Joshua and of the elders who outlived him and who had seen all the great things the Lord had done for Israel." But time passed, and the day came when the power of God was forgotten: "After that whole generation had been gathered to their fathers, another generation grew up, who knew neither the Lord nor what he had done for Israel" (2:10). The result was almost inevitable as the people subverted the Lord's authority: "Then the Israelites did evil in the eyes of the Lord and served the Baals. They forsook the Lord, the God of their fathers, who had brought them out of Egypt. They followed and worshiped various gods of the peoples around them. They provoked the Lord to anger because they forsook him and served Baal and the Ashteroths" (2:11-13).

Another very poignant example of the relationship between authority and power in Judges is found in chapter 13 and the account of the angelic appearance to Manoah and his wife in anticipation of the miraculous conception and birth of their son, Samson. When his wife first reported the angelic manifestation to Manoah, she said in 13:6, "A man of God came to me. He looked like an angel of God, very awesome." When Manoah himself later saw the angel and wanted to provide food for the angel, he was told according to 13:16, "Even though you detain me, I will not eat any of your food. But if you prepare a burnt offering, offer it to the Lord." Failing to understand the angelical authority, Manoah asked the angel's name, and the angel replied, "Why do you ask my name? It is beyond understanding"

(13:18). When Manoah made a burnt offering as directed, 13:19 says, "And the Lord did an amazing thing while Manoah and his wife watched [the NASB says, "He performed wonders while Manoah and his wife looked on."] Then 13:20 adds, "As the flame blazed up from the altar toward heaven, the angel of the Lord ascended in the flame" so that "Manoah and his wife fell with their faces to the ground," and "Manoah realized that it was the angel of the Lord." In utter fear of his new understanding, Manoah said in 13:22, "We are doomed to die! . . . We have seen God!" Thus the power displayed in the manifestation produced understanding and respect for the angelic or divine authority.

## 1 Samuel

The birth of Samuel as recounted in 1 Samuel 1 also provided occasion for the association of power and authority in relationship to God's dealings with Israel. Hannah's ability to conceive and bear a son seems miraculous enough, as a result of prayer and the direct intervention of God. So Hannah said in 1 Samuel 1:20 that she named her son Samuel, "because I asked the Lord for him." In her prayer of thanksgiving (1 Samuel 2:1-10), Hannah exalted the Lord: "There is no one holy like the Lord; there is no one besides you; there is no Rock like our God" (2:2).

Throughout 1 and 2 Samuel we see how the vicissitudes of war and personal conflict produced opportunity for the power of God to be demonstrated to the end that the Lord's authority might be honored. When the Philistines defeated the Israelites and captured the ark of the covenant according to 1 Samuel 4, both the Philistines and the Israelites realized the significance of what had taken place. The Philistines seemed to have a healthy respect for the ark of the Lord and the divine power it represented when the Israelites brought the ark into their camp, a respect brought about by the mighty acts done by God (or "gods" as the Philistines believed). According to 1 Samuel 4 the Philistines said, "A god has come into the camp . . . We're in trouble! Nothing like this has happened before. Woe to us! Who will deliver us from the hand of these mighty gods? They are the gods who struck the Egyptians with all kinds of plagues in the desert" (4:7-8). 4:21-22 indicates that after the Philistines captured the ark, and both Eli and Phineas had died, Eli's daughter-in-law, the wife of Phineas, named her newborn son "Ichabod." The text quotes her as saying, "The glory has departed from Israel," and explains that it was "because of the capture of the ark of God and the deaths of her father-in-law and her husband. She said, 'The glory has departed from Israel, for the ark of God has been captured.'"

The vicissitudes of Israel's struggles with its enemies demonstrate the importance of the relationship between the authority of God and His power in providing help to Israel in the nation's struggles. When the people demanded a king for themselves, they were warned that the authority of God was in danger of being rejected, and that such rejection would lead to God's power being withdrawn from the nation. So in 1 Samuel 12:14-15, Samuel said, "If you fear the Lord and serve and obey him and do not rebel against his commands, and if both you and the king who reigns over you follow the Lord your God—good! But if you do not obey the Lord, and if you rebel against his commands, his hand will be against you, at it was against your fathers."

This speech of Samuel not only warned that the power of God might turn against Israel, but it was followed by a demonstration of such power. Samuel said in 12:16-17, "Now then, stand still and see this great thing the Lord is about to do before your eyes! Is it not wheat harvest now? I will call upon the Lord to send thunder and rain. And you will realize what an evil thing you did in the eyes of the Lord when you asked for a king." Then Samuel did as he warned. He called upon the Lord, and "that same day the Lord sent thunder and rain. So all the people stood in awe of the Lord and of Samuel" (12:18).

Samuel continued to emphasize the significance of the Lord's authority. He said in 12:22, "For the sake of his great name the Lord will not reject his people, because the Lord was pleased to make you his own." He also warned that the power of God which had made Israel great could be withdrawn in order to effect the fall of the nation: "But be sure to fear the Lord and serve him faithfully with all your heart; consider what great things he has done for you. Yet if you persist in doing evil, both you and your king will be swept away" (12:24-25).

This sets the tone for the rest of the books of Samuel as well as the books of Kings. God's authority is emphasized repeatedly in various ways, and His power is demonstrated variously in the life of the nation of Israel. Such is the case in regard to the struggle with the Philistines and particularly with its champion, Goliath, as noted in the introductory chapter.

The failure of Saul as king also provided an opportunity for demonstrating the authority-power connection. According to 1 Samuel 28, when Saul consulted the witch of Endor, she conjured up Samuel who laid blame for Saul's failure at the king's refusal to heed the authority of the Lord. Samuel said in 28:18, "Because you did not obey the Lord or carry out his fierce wrath against the Amalekites, the Lord has done this to you today." And in 28:19 Samuel indicated how the power of God would enforce His authority: "The Lord will hand over both Israel and you to the Philistines, and tomorrow you and your sons will be with me. The Lord will also hand over the army of Israel to the Philistines."

## 2 Samuel

The death of Uzzah (2 Samuel 6:7) in the course of moving the ark of God from Baalah/Kiriath Jearim to Jerusalem also underscored the authority-power connection. By the time of David there was a long-standing prohibition against touching the ark or other implements of the Tent of Meeting. So Numbers 4:15 says, "The Kohathites are to come to do the carrying. But they must not touch the holy things or they will die." According to 2

Samuel 6:6, Uzzah violated this command: "Uzzah reached out and took hold of the ark of God, because the oxen stumbled." The power of the Lord was then displayed according to 6:7: "The Lord's anger burned against Uzzah because of his irreverent act; therefore God struck him down and he died there beside the ark of God." The effect was immediate so far as David was concerned: "David was angry because the Lord's wrath had broken out against Uzzah" (6:8). It also produced a sobering reality in David: "David was afraid of the Lord that day and said, 'How can the ark of the Lord ever come to me?' He was not willing to take the ark of the Lord to be with him in the City of David" (6:9-10). So for three months the ark blessed the house of Obed-Edom where it had been left, until David finally brought the ark to Jerusalem.

The authority and power of God are also an issue in regard to David's affair with Bathsheba, and the death of Bathsheba's husband Uriah. When Nathan confronted David about David's sin, the issue of the Lord's authority was in sharp focus. Nathan said, "You are the man! This is what the Lord, the God of Israel, says: 'I anointed you king over Israel, and I delivered you from the hand of Saul. I gave your master's house to you, and your master's wives into your arms. I gave you the house of Israel and Judah. And if all this had been too little, I would have given you even more. Why did you despise the word of the Lord by doing what is evil in his eyes?'" (2 Samuel 12:7-9). The power of God then brought punishment to David who was told, "Out of your own household I am going to bring calamity upon you. Before your very eyes I will take your wives and give them to one who is close to you, and he will lie with your wives in broad daylight" (12:11). And Nathan also prophesied that "the son born to you will die" (12:14). Thus God's power brought judgment to pass because of David's despising of the Lord's authority.

## 1 Kings

The reign of Solomon provides opportunity for the authority of God to be linked to His power. In 1 Kings 9, in conjunction with the dedication of the temple, we read how the Lord tied rejection of His authority to Israel's own national downfall. In 9:3 the Lord said, "I have consecrated this temple, which you have built, by putting my Name there forever. My eyes and my heart will always be there." 9:4 continues, "If you walk before me in integrity of heart . . . and do all I command and observe my decrees and laws, I will establish your royal throne over Israel forever." Then this word of authority turns to one of power through punishment in 9:6-9: "If you or your sons turn away from me and do not observe the commands and decrees I have given you and go off to serve other gods and worship them, then I will cut off Israel from the land I have given them and will reject this temple I have consecrated for my Name. Israel will then become a byword and an object of ridicule among all peoples." The word continues: "All who pass by will be appalled and will scoff and say, 'Why has the Lord done such a thing to this land and to this temple?'" And the reply will be, "Because they have forsaken the Lord their God, who brought their fathers out of Egypt, and have embraced other gods, worshiping and serving them—that is why the Lord brought all this disaster on them."

The unusual incident in 1 Kings 13 concerning a disobedient man of God or prophet and a lying prophet also demonstrates the relationship between authority and power. The disobedient man of God who was from Judah went to Bethel and prophesied there by the word of the Lord concerning King Jeroboam and the splitting of the altar in Bethel. He started back to Judah, but being obedient to the word of the Lord headed home by a different way than which he had gone to Bethel, also being forbidden to eat bread or drink water as he went. The lying prophet met him and persuaded him to go home with him to eat bread and drink water. The result was that the man of God disobeyed the authority of the Lord, even as the lying prophet said in 1 Kings 13:21: "This is what the Lord says: 'You have defied the word of the Lord and have not kept the command the Lord your God gave you.'" Then the power of God was evident in the punishment that came to the disobedient man of God who was killed by a lion, as the lying prophet said in 13:26: "The Lord has given him over to the lion, which has mauled him and killed him, as the word of the Lord had warned him."

In the events associated with the prophet Elijah as recorded in 1 Kings, perhaps none is more significant for the authority-power connection than that of Elijah's confrontation with prophets of Baal at Mount Carmel in 1 Kings 18. When it came time for Elijah to offer his sacrifice on the altar that had been built there, Elijah prayed for fire to fall from God to the altar and spoke specifically concerning the Lord's authority according to 18:36-37: "O Lord, God of Abraham, Isaac and Israel, let it be known today that you are God in Israel and that I am your servant and have done all these things at your command. Answer me, O Lord, answer me, so these people will know that you, O Lord, are God, and that you are turning their hearts back again." The result was a demonstration of God's power: "The fire of the Lord fell and burned up the sacrifice, the wood, the stones and the soil, and also licked up the water in the trench" (18:38). And the effect was immediate, as the people cried, "The Lord—he is God! The Lord—he is God!"

Another unusual demonstration of power in conjunction with the Lord's authority is found in 1 Kings 20:35-43. In the larger context of 1 Kings 20, Israel's king Ahab had allowed the Aramean king Ben-Hadad to go free when Ben-Hadad's destruction was easily at hand. One prophet, speaking by the word of the Lord, told another to hit him: "Strike me with your weapon" (20:35). The other prophet refused to do so. The prophet who made the demand then said, "Because you have not obeyed the Lord, as soon as you leave me a lion will kill you," and the result was that "after the man went away, a lion found him and killed him" (20:36). The prophet then found another prophet who did indeed strike him. In this wounded condition and in disguise, the prophet then gained access to Ahab. He tied Ahab's refusal to heed the Lord's authority in regard to the destruction of the Arameans and Ben-Hadad to God's power in the future defeat of Ahab and Israel as well as Ahab's death: "He said to the king, 'This is what the Lord says: "You have set free a man I had determined should die. Therefore it is your life for his life, your people for his people"'" (20:42).

Ahab's demise was also prophesied by Elijah (1 Kings 21:17-24), in connection with Ahab's misappropriation of Naboth's vineyard, and by the prophet Micaiah. In the latter case there is a direct connection between the Lord's authority and power as found in 1 King 22. When the two kings, Ahab of Israel and Jehoshaphat of Judah, joined forces to fight the Arameans, the King of Judah urged Ahab to seek the prophetic word of the Lord even though Ahab had already been assured by four hundred other prophets that he would succeed (see 1 Kings 22:5-6). Micaiah was consulted and predicted disastrous consequences for Ahab since Micaiah had received a vision according to which a lying spirit had been put into the mouths of the prophets who prophesied in favor of Ahab. When Ahab ordered Micaiah to be imprisoned, Micaiah said to Ahab in 22:28, "If you ever return safely, the Lord has not spoken through me," and he added, "Mark my words, all you people." Ahab died in battle according to 22:29-40, thus vindicating God's authority as proclaimed by the true prophets, or according to 22:38, "as the word of the Lord had declared." Once again, God's power enforced His authority.

## 2 Kings

Of the many miracles of Elisha, one in particular seems to address the relationship between God's authority and power. 2 Kings 6 tells of Israel's struggles with the Arameans and their king Ben-Hadad, and how the residents of Samaria virtually starved when their city was besieged by the Arameans. Then in 2 Kings 7:1, Elisha prophesied that on the following day there would be plenty of food: "This is what the Lord says: About this time tomorrow, a seah of flour will sell for a shekel and two seahs of barley for a shekel at the gate of Samaria." King Joram's personal officer was incredulous and said to Elisha according to 7:2, "Look, even if the Lord should open the floodgates of the heavens, could this happen?" And Elisha replied, "You will see it with your own eyes . . . but you will not eat any of it." The Lord then caused the invading Arameans to hastily flee their camp site while leaving their provisions and possessions behind. When Joram's officers went to investigate, 7:15 says, "They found the whole road strewn with the clothing and equipment the Arameans had thrown away in their headlong flight," and 7:16 says that "the people went out and plundered the camp of the Arameans. So a seah of flour sold for a shekel, and two seahs of barley sold for a shekel, as the Lord had said." 7:17 adds that the king's officer died, "just as the man of God had foretold," and 7:18 says, "It happened as the man of God had said to the king."

The execution of the sons of Ahab at the direction of Jehu may also be regarded as evidence of the power of God wielded in response to the authority of God. According to 2 Kings 10, seventy sons of Ahab were executed. Jehu addressed his people and assessed the situation as 10:9 says: "You are innocent. It was I who conspired against my master and killed him, but who killed all these? Know then, that not a word the Lord has spoken against the house of Ahab will fail. The Lord has done what he promised through his servant Elijah." Then Jehu had other members of the house of Ahab killed, including those who lived in Jezreel (10:11), those whom he met at Beth Eked (10:14), and those who were still in Samaria as 10:17 says: "When Jehu came to Samaria, he killed all who were left there of Ahab's family; he destroyed them, according to the word of the Lord spoken to Elijah." The word or authority of the Lord was affirmed by the destruction of Ahab's family.

2 Kings 17 records how Assyria prevailed against the kingdom of Israel and its capital, Samaria. 17:5 says, "The king of Assyria invaded the entire land, marched against Samaria and laid siege to it for three years." There follows in 17:7-23 a kind of historical review of Israel's and Judah's contempt for the Lord's authority, and also how the Lord's punishment served as a demonstration of the Lord's power in response to the rejection of His authority. 17:7 says, "All this took place because the Israelites had sinned against the Lord their God, who had brought them up out of Egypt from under the power of Pharaoh king of Egypt." A virtual litany of examples showing Israel's rejection of God's authority follows. 17:18 then asserts, "So the Lord was very angry with Israel and removed them from his presence;" 17:20 adds, "Therefore the Lord rejected all the people of Israel; he afflicted them and gave them into the hands of plunderers, until he thrust them from his presence;" and 17:23 concludes, "The Lord removed them from his presence, as he had warned through all his servants the prophets."

The failure to recognize and honor the Lord's authority brought continued affliction even to the displaced people whom the Assyrians sent to inhabit the cities of Israel/Samaria. God's punishing power was unleashed in an unusual way, as 17:25 says: "When they first lived there, they did not worship the Lord; so he sent lions among them and they killed some of the people." Chapter 17 goes on to tell how the king of Assyria had an exiled priest from Samaria sent back to Israel to help the displaced people there understand what God required. So, as 17:28 says, "One of the priests who had been exiled from Samaria came to live in Bethel and taught them how to worship the Lord." However, this did not solve the problem but resulted in a syncretistic religious practice, as 17:33 indicates: "They worshiped the Lord, but they also served their own gods in accordance with the customs of the nations from which they had been brought."

2 Kings 17 goes on to contrast the authority and power of God as displayed in the exodus from Egypt with Israel's failure to stand against its enemies. 17:36 says, "But the Lord, who brought you up out of Egypt with mighty power and outstretched arm, is the one you must worship. To him you shall bow down and to him offer sacrifices." And 17:39 adds, "Rather,

worship the Lord your God; it is he who will deliver you from the hand of all your enemies."

2 Kings 18 notes specifically that Judah fared somewhat better than Israel because of Hezekiah's reforms as well as his regard for the Lord's authority. So 18:5-6 says that Hezekiah "trusted in the Lord, the God of Israel . . . He held fast to the Lord and did not cease to follow him; he kept the commands the Lord had given to Moses." The result was that God's power worked for Hezekiah, as 18:7-8 says: "And the Lord was with him; he was successful in whatever he undertook. He rebelled against the king of Assyria and did not serve him. From watchtower to fortified city, he defeated the Philistines, as far as Gaza and its territory." By way of contrast, 18:11 says of Israel, "The king of Assyria deported Israel to Assyria and settled them in Halah, in Gozan on the Habor River and in towns of the Medes." The reason? God's power was being demonstrated in the face of the rejection of His authority, as 18:12 says: "Because they had not obeyed the Lord their God, but had violated his covenant—all that Moses the servant of the Lord commanded. They neither listened to the commands nor carried them out." Hezekiah's prayer (19:14-19) culminated in this request for deliverance from the Assyrians and their king Sennacherib that associates the authority and power of the Lord: "Now, O Lord our God, deliver us from his hand, so that all kingdoms on earth may know that you alone, O Lord, are God."

Even Hezekiah's deathly illness (2 Kings 20:1-11) became an occasion for the authority and power of God to be recognized and demonstrated. In the presence of Isaiah the prophet, Hezekiah prayed for change in the course of his sickness while asking the Lord to remember how he had respected the authority of the Lord. When Isaiah received divine word that the life of Hezekiah would be extended by fifteen years, Hezekiah sought proof that it would indeed be as Isaiah said. As a sign of God's power, and in response to Hezekiah's request, the shadow on the stairs of the king's palace moved backwards and up ten steps. But ominous anticipation continued to haunt Hezekiah's reign, and Isaiah later said to the king: "Hear the word of the Lord: The time will surely come when everything in your palace, and all that your fathers have stored up until this day, will be carried off to Babylon. Nothing will be left, says the Lord. And some of your descendants, your own flesh and blood, that will be born to you, will be taken away, and they will become eunuchs in the palace of the king of Babylon" (20:16-18). So the power of God would continue to be demonstrated through Israel's/Judah's fall in the face of the rejection of God's authority.

Manasseh's reign, as described in 2 Kings 21:1-18, brought the issue of authority and power to a head. His rejection of the authority of God surfaced in many ways, including the fact that he built altars to various gods and starry hosts in the temple at Jerusalem, the very temple of which the Lord said, "In Jerusalem I will put my Name" (21:4 and 7). So the power of God was to be unleashed, as the Lord spoke through His servants, the prophets, according to 21:12-15: "Therefore this is what the Lord, the God of Israel, says: I am going to bring such disaster on Jerusalem and Judah that the ears of everyone who hears of it will tingle. I will stretch out over Jerusalem the measuring line used against Samaria and the plumb line used against the house of Ahab." The word continues, "I will wipe out Jerusalem as one wipes a dish, wiping it and turning it upside down. I will forsake the remnant of my inheritance and hand them over to their enemies. They will be looted and plundered by all their foes, because they have done evil in my eyes and have provoked me to anger from the day their forefathers came out of Egypt until this day."

Even though the reign of Josiah brought some restoration of respect for divine authority, the discovery of a lost book of the law brought a sense of the inevitability of God's power being unleashed in punishment. Thus in 2 Kings 22:13, Josiah said, "Great is the Lord's anger that burns against us, because our fathers have not obeyed the words of this book; they have not acted in accordance with all that is written there concerning us." This word was reinforced by Huldah, the prophetess, in 22:15-20, as she brought the authority and power of God into sharp focus: "This is what the Lord says: I am going to bring disaster on this place and its people, according to everything written in the book the king of Judah has read. Because they have forsaken me and burned incense to other gods and provoked me to anger by all the idols their hands have made, my anger will burn against this place and will not be quenched."

Although Josiah instituted significant reforms as we read in 2 Kings 23, a final word of authority and power is found in 23:26-27: "Nevertheless, the Lord did not turn away from the heat of his fierce anger, which burned against Judah because of all that Manasseh had done to provoke him to anger. So the Lord said, 'I will remove Judah also from my presence as I removed Israel, and I will reject Jerusalem, the city I chose, and this temple about which I said, "There shall my Name be."'"

# Chapter 9

# The Old Testament—Authority and Power in God's Mighty Acts

## The Major Prophets

The prophetic literature is filled with references to divine authority. As we have seen, such concern for authority often occurs in conjunction with references to the power of God as displayed in creation or various created realities. The prophetic literature also relates the authority of God to the power of God as demonstrated in His might acts, especially those acts which involve national and international conflicts. A rather constant prophetic theme finds the power of God displayed in the fate of the nations, including Israel and Judah, especially as the nations recognize or reject God's authority. The passages that follow from the major prophets, Isaiah, Jeremiah, and Ezekiel, are exemplary only and should not be regarded as exhaustive of the possible examples.

### Isaiah

Isaiah 8 warns that rejection of the Lord's authority will bring God's power unleashed in calamity, in this case the calamity of Assyria flowing like a river. So 8:7-8 says, "The Lord is about to bring against them the mighty floodwaters of the River—the king of Assyria with all his pomp. It will overflow all its channels, run over all its banks and sweep on into Judah, swirling over it, passing through it and reaching up to the neck." Isaiah asserts the Lord's authority in 8:13-14: "The Lord Almighty is the one you are to regard as holy, he is the one you are to fear, he is the one you are to dread, and he will be a sanctuary." Then in 8:18 Isaiah says, "Here am I, and the children the Lord has given me. We are signs and symbols in Israel from the Lord Almighty, who dwells on Mount Zion." And what of those who inquire of mediums and spiritists, but not their God, those who ignore the law and testimony of God? 8:21-22 says, "They will roam through the land . . . they will become enraged and . . . will curse their king and their God. Then they will look toward the earth and see only distress and darkness and fearful gloom, and they will be thrust into utter darkness."

As Isaiah continues, there are many references to the powerful acts of God which bring judgment or punishment to the earth and lead to calls for honoring divine authority. So Isaiah 24:1-3 says, "See, the Lord is going to lay waste the earth and devastate it; he will ruin its face and scatter its inhabitants . . . The earth will be completely laid waste and totally plundered. The Lord has spoken this word." Then in 24:14-16 comes more recognition of God's authority: "They raise their voices, they shout for joy; from the west they acclaim the Lord's majesty. Therefore in the east give glory to the Lord; exalt the name of the Lord, the God of Israel, in the islands of the sea. From the ends of the earth we hear singing: 'Glory to the Righteous One.'" This is followed in 25:1-2 by words which exalt the Lord and again recognize His power: "O Lord, you are my God; I will exalt you and praise your name, for in perfect faithfulness you have done marvelous things, things planned long ago. You have made the city a heap of rubble, the fortified town a ruin, the foreigners' stronghold a city no more; it will never be rebuilt."

The subsequent chapters of Isaiah, so filled with recognition of the Lord's authority and creative power as we have previously noted, do not neglect the association of authority and mighty acts. Thus Isaiah 59:18 says, "According to what they have done, so will he repay wrath to his enemies and retribution to his foes; he will repay the islands their due." Then 59:19 continues, "From the west, men will fear the name of the Lord, and from the rising of the sun, they will revere his glory." Isaiah's last chapter 66 also associates the powerful acts and authority of the Lord, as in verse 4, "So I also will choose harsh treatment for them and will bring upon them what they dread. For when I called, no one answered, when I spoke, no one listened," and in verse 5, "Let the Lord be glorified, that we may see your joy! Yet they will be put to shame."

## Jeremiah

The authority of God and His power as displayed in mighty acts are also found closely linked in the prophet Jeremiah. Such acts often speak of the punishment that awaits Judah/Jerusalem at the hand of the Babylonians. Several passages are especially notable.

Jeremiah 3 is a good starting point. Here the prophet points to Israel's faithlessness, while urging Israel to return to God. Israel's failure nationally is due to its failure to honor the Lord. So 3:25 says, "Let us lie down in our shame, and let our disgrace cover us. We have sinned against the Lord our God, both we and our fathers; from our youth till this day we have not obeyed the Lord our God." Then in 5:18-19, the Lord declares, "Yet even in those days . . . I will not destroy you completely. And when the people ask, 'Why has the Lord our God done all this to us?' you will tell them, 'As you have forsaken me and served foreign gods in your own land, so now you will serve foreigners in a land not your own.'"

Jeremiah also associates the authority of the Lord with God's punishing power in chapter 22. There it is Judah and the evil kings who sit upon the throne of David who are in focus. Thus in 22:8-9 the Lord says, "People from many nations will pass by this city and will ask one another, 'Why has the Lord done such a thing to this great city?' And the answer will be: 'Because they have forsaken the covenant of the Lord their God and have worshipped and served other gods.'"

In Jeremiah 23, the outlook is much different. It is the Lord's willingness to deliver Israel that will prove to be both a demonstration of His power and a testimony to His authority. So according to 23:3 the Lord says, "I myself will gather the remnant of my flock out of all the countries where I have driven them and will bring them back to their pasture, where they will be fruitful and increase in number." In accomplishing this, the Lord promises to raise a "righteous Branch" or "King" who will not only reign justly but will be called, "The Lord Our Righteousness" (23:5-6). And then the Lord adds in 23:7-8: "So, then, the days are coming . . . when people will no longer say, 'As surely as the Lord lives, who brought the Israelites up out of Egypt,' but they will say, 'As surely as the Lord lives, who brought the descendants of Israel up out of the land of the north and out of all the countries where he had banished them.'"

Jeremiah 25 contains the prophecy of seventy years of Babylonian captivity, and the authority and power of God are in clear proximity here. In 25:8-11, the Lord Almighty says, "Because you have not listened to my words, I will summon all the people of the north and my servant Nebuchadnezzar king of Babylon . . . and I will bring them against this land and its inhabitants and against all the surrounding nations. I will completely destroy them . . . This whole country will become a desolate wasteland, and these nations will serve the king of Babylon seventy years."

Jeremiah's prayer in chapter 32 associates the authority of the Lord with both His creative power and the power of His mighty acts. Thus 32:17 says, "Ah, Sovereign Lord, you have made the heavens and the earth by your great power and outstretched arm. Nothing is too hard for you." Then Jeremiah continues in 32:18-19, "O great and powerful God, whose name is the Lord Almighty, great are your purposes and mighty are your deeds." 32:20 adds, "You performed miraculous signs and wonders in Egypt and have continued them to this day, both in Israel and among all mankind, and have gained the renown that is still yours." Jeremiah's prayer continues in similar fashion until the word of the Lord comes to Jeremiah, according to 32:27: "I am the Lord, the God of all mankind. Is anything too hard for me?"

Jeremiah's association of authority and power continues to be seen in a number of passages. In chapter 44 a warning goes out to Jews who have taken refuge in Egypt. 44:2-3 says, "This is what the Lord Almighty, the God of Israel, says: You saw the great disaster I brought on Jerusalem and on all the towns of Judah. Today they lie deserted and in ruins because of the evil they have done. They provoked me to anger by burning incense and by worshiping other gods that neither they nor you nor your fathers ever knew." This tone continues throughout the chapter as the issue of refuge in Egypt casts a heavy shadow. So the word of the Lord says in 44:26-27, "I swear by my great name . . . that no one from Judah living anywhere in Egypt will ever again invoke my name or swear, 'As surely as the Sovereign Lord lives.' For I am watching over them for harm, not for good." And in 44:29 the Lord adds, "This will be a sign to you that I will punish you in this place . . . so that you will know that my threats of harm against you will surely stand . . . I am going to hand Pharaoh Hophra king of Egypt over to his enemies who seek his life, just as I handed Zedekiah king of Judah over to Nebuchadnezzar king of Babylon, the enemy who was seeking his life."

## Ezekiel

None of the prophetic books, and perhaps no book of the entire Bible, is so committed to demonstrating the authority of God by His mighty acts as is Ezekiel. Again and again, some sixty times from chapter 5 to chapter 39, the Lord asserts His authority by saying through Ezekiel that either "you" or "they" will know, and usually what will be known is "that I am the Lord." Thus Ezekiel's vision in chapter 1 moves to what is called "the appearance of the likeness of the glory of the Lord" (1:28). There follow in chapters 2-4 the call of Ezekiel as well as directions for the prophet's message to Israel/Jerusalem. In this context there emerges a series of punishments which are to fall upon God's people including the following: "In this way the people of Israel will eat defiled food among the nations where I will drive them" (4:13); "I will inflict punishment on you and will scatter all your survivors to the winds" (5:10); and "I myself will withdraw my favor; I will not look on you with pity or spare you" (5:11). This leads to the inevitable conclusion in 5:13: "And when I have spent my wrath upon them, they will know that I the Lord have spoken in my zeal."

Chapter 6 unleashes more of this prophetic word of punishment so that 6:7 says, "Your people will fall slain among you, and you will know that I am the Lord." Then 6:10 continues, "And they will know that I am the Lord; I did not threaten in vain to bring this calamity on them." 6:13 persists: "And they will know that I am the Lord, when their people lie slain among their idols around their altars . . . places where they offered fragrant incense to all their idols." So 6:14 concludes, "And I will stretch out my hands against them and make the land a desolate waste . . . Then they will know that I am the Lord."

Ezekiel continues largely in this vein until just before his temple vision in chapters 40-48. At the close of chapter 37, the prophecy of the restoration of the Davidic kingdom concludes as follows in 37:26-28: "I will make a covenant of peace with them; it will be an everlasting covenant... and I will put my sanctuary among them forever. My dwelling place will be with them; I will be their God, and they will be my people. Then the nations will know that I the Lord make Israel holy, when my sanctuary is among them forever."

Ezekiel 38-39 then turns to prophecy concerning the defeat of Gog and Magog, prophecy that also exalts the Lord while speaking of His acts of judgment. 38:23 says, "And so I will show my greatness and my holiness, and I will make myself known in the sight of many nations. Then they will know that I am the Lord." In similar fashion, the Lord says in 39:1, " I am against you, O Gog," while 39:6 adds, "I will send fire on Magog and on those who live in safety in the coastlands," with the result that "they will know that I am the Lord." 39:21-22 then persists in this view: "I will display my glory among the nations, and all the nations will see the punishment I inflict and the hand I lay upon them. From that day forward the house of Israel will know that I am the Lord their God." Finally, in 39:25 the Lord says, "I will now bring Jacob back from captivity and will have compassion on all the people of Israel, and I will be zealous for my holy name." This is to the end that "when I have brought them back from the nations and have gathered them from the countries of their enemies, I will show myself holy through them in the sight of many nations. Then they will know that I am the Lord their God" (39:27-28).

# Chapter 10

# The Old Testament - Authority and Power in God's Mighty Acts

## The Minor Prophets (Hosea – Malachi)

The minor prophets also refer extensively to divine authority, and they relate such authority to the power of God, especially the power of God as demonstrated in mighty acts which involve national and international conflicts. As with the major prophets, the examples that follow from the minor prophets are exemplary only.

### Hosea

Hosea is filled with divine threats concerning Israel's and Samaria's national security. The constant warning is that God will bring punishment to Israel for its failure to be responsive to His authority. So in Hosea 1:4-5 the Lord says, in regard to Hosea's son, "Call him Jezreel, because I will soon punish the house of Jehu for the massacre at Jezreel, and I will put an end to the kingdom of Israel. In that day I will break Israel's bow in the Valley of Jezreel."

Hosea 4 contains God's case or lawsuit against Israel, and 4:1 asserts His authority: "Hear the word of the Lord, you Israelites, because the Lord has a charge to bring against you who live in the land: 'There is no faithfulness, no love, no acknowledgment of God in the land.'" A mixture of authority and power through punishment then follows. 4:6 says, "Because you have rejected knowledge, I also reject you as my priests; because you have ignored the law of your God, I also will ignore your children." Then 4:9 adds, "And it will be: Like people, like priests. I will punish both of them for their ways and repay them for their deeds." 4:19 concludes, "A whirlwind will sweep them away, and their sacrifices will bring them shame."

Chapter 8 also weaves together the message of God's authority and power. 8:1 says, "An eagle is over the house of the Lord because the people have broken my covenant and rebelled against my law." 8:4 continues, "They set up kings without my consent; they choose princes without my approval," and 8:7-9 adds, "They sow the wind and reap the whirlwind . . . Israel is swallowed up; now she is among the nations like a worthless thing. For they have gone up to Assyria like a wild donkey wandering alone." In 8:13, the prophet says "the Lord is not pleased with them. Now he will remember their wickedness and punish their sins: They will return to Egypt," and the Lord adds in 8:14, "But I will send fire upon their cities that will consume their fortresses."

## Joel

Joel exalts the authority of the Lord in a variety of ways, notably in reference to the day of the Lord, as in 2:11: "The Lord thunders at the head of his army; his forces are beyond number, and mighty are those who obey his command. The day of the Lord is great; it is dreadful. Who can endure it?" The Lord's power is seen in the destruction and defeat that accompanies the day of the Lord, and is regarded both literally and figuratively as in 2:3: "Before them fire devours, behind them a flame blazes. Before them the land is like the garden of Eden, behind them, a desert waste—nothing escapes them;" and in 2:10: "Before them the earth shakes, the sky trembles, the sun and moon are darkened, and the stars no longer shine."

Joel's regard for the authority and power of the Lord is also seen in the way that God restores the fortunes of His people. So 3:1 says, "In those days and at that time, when I restore the fortunes of Judah and Jerusalem, I will gather all nations and bring them down to the Valley of Jehoshaphat. There I will enter into judgment against them concerning my inheritance, my people Israel, for they scattered my people among the nations and divided up my land." 3:16 then adds, "The Lord will roar from Zion and thunder from Jerusalem; the earth and the sky will tremble. But the Lord will be a refuge for his people, a stronghold for the people of Israel." And 3:20-21 concludes, "Judah will be inhabited forever and Jerusalem through all generations. Their bloodguilt, which I have not pardoned, I will pardon. The Lord dwells in Zion!"

## Amos

Amos likewise is concerned with the power of God unleashed in the punishment of the nations, and the use of such power is designed to demonstrate the Lord's authority. So, for example, Amos 3:13-14 says, "'Hear this and testify against the house of Jacob,' declares the Lord, the Lord God Almighty. 'On the day I punish Israel for her sins, I will destroy the altars of Bethel; the horns of the altar will be cut off and fall to the ground.'" Then 4:2 adds, "The Sovereign Lord has sworn by his holiness: 'The time will surely come when you will be taken away with hooks, the last of you with fishhooks.'" Chapter 4 continues with a series of divine judgments evidencing the power of God: "I gave you empty stomachs in every city and lack of bread in every town" (4:6); "I also withheld rain from you" (4:7); "Many times I struck your gardens and vineyards, I struck them with blight and mildew" (4:9); "I sent plagues among you as I did to Egypt. I killed your young men with the sword, along with your captured horses" (4:10); "I overthrew some of you as I overthrew Sodom and Gomorrah" (4:11). And following each item in this series, the Lord declares, "Yet you have not returned to me." 4:12-13 concludes with this word from the Lord: "Therefore this is what I will do to you, Israel, and because I will do this to you, prepare to meet your God, O Israel."

## Jonah

Jonah clearly associates the authority and power of the Lord in connection with Jonah's refusal to go to Nineveh to declare the Lord's word as the Lord directed, and the resulting peril of the ship on which Jonah was fleeing (1:1-3). The Lord sent a great wind on the sea, and Jonah's response to the sailors who questioned their calamity is stated in 1:9: "I am a Hebrew and I worship the Lord, the God of heaven, who made the sea and the land." Later, after Jonah had been swallowed by a great fish, his prayer showed this kind of response: "You hurled me into the deep, into the very heart of the seas, and the currents swirled about me . . . I said, 'I have been banished from your sight'. . . But you brought my life up from the pit, O Lord my God . . . Salvation comes the Lord" (2:1-9).

## Micah

Micah's association of authority and power is apparent almost immediately as his book opens. Micah 1:2 says, "Hear, O peoples, all of you, listen, O earth and all who are in it, that the Sovereign Lord may witness against you, the Lord from his holy temple." Then 1:3 adds, "Look! The Lord is coming from his dwelling place; he comes down and treads the high places of the earth." There follow words of the punishment that the Lord brings upon his own people, as in 1:6: "Therefore I will make Samaria a heap of rubble; a place for planting vineyards. I will pour her stones into the valley and lay bare her foundations." Very pointedly, 1:12 adds that "disaster has come from the Lord, even to the gate of Jerusalem." And when the Lord's words against false prophets conclude, he says in 3:12, "Therefore, because of you, Zion will be plowed like a field, Jerusalem will become a heap of rubble, the temple hill a mound overgrown with thickets." But God's authority and power are also seen in His compassion, as 7:18 says: "Who is a God like you, who pardons sin and forgives the transgression of the remnant of his inheritance? You do not stay angry forever but delight to show mercy."

## Nahum

Nahum also refers to the authority and power of the Lord from the beginning of his work concerning Nineveh. Nahum 1:2 says, "The Lord is a jealous and avenging God; the Lord takes vengeance and is filled with wrath. The Lord takes vengeance on his foes and maintains his wrath against his enemies." In the midst of the prophetic word of punishment against Nineveh, the Lord Almighty says in 2:13, "I am against you . . . I will burn up your chariots in smoke, and the sword will devour your young lions. I will leave you no prey on the earth. The voices of your messengers will no longer be heard."

## Habakkuk

Habakkuk also relates the authority and power of God, especially in terms of the punishment to be carried out by the Babylonians. Thus Habakkuk 1:12 says, "O Lord, are you not from everlasting? My God, my Holy One, we will not die. O Lord, you have appointed them to execute judgment; O Rock, you have ordained them to punish." The prophet's prayer in chapter 3 also shows the connection. 3:1 says, "Lord, I have heard of your fame; I stand in awe of your deeds, O Lord," and 3:3 continues, "God comes from Teman, and the Holy One from Mount Paran. His glory covered the heavens, and his praise filled the earth." Then 3:5-6 adds, "Plague went before him; pestilence followed his steps. He stood, and shook the earth; he looked and made the nations tremble."

## Zephaniah

Zephaniah, like Joel and Amos, has a certain fascination with "the day of the Lord," and in this connection he has high regard for the authority of the Lord. So Zephaniah 3:15, offering hope, says, "The Lord has taken away your punishment, he has turned back your enemy. The Lord, the King of Israel, is with you; never again will you fear any harm." Then 3:17 adds, "The Lord your God is with you, he is mighty to save." But Zephaniah is more concerned about the fact that the power of God is demonstrated in judgment against nations. Of the Philistines, for instance, he says in 2:4-5, "Gaza will be abandoned and Ashkelon left in ruins. At midday Ashdod will be emptied and Ekron uprooted. Woe to you who live by the sea, O Kerethite people; the word of the Lord is against you, O Canaan, land of the Philistines. I will destroy you, and none will be left." Later, in 2:9, the Lord warns, "Therefore, as surely as I live 'declares the Lord Almighty, the God of Israel,' surely Moab will become like Sodom, the Ammonites like Gomorrah —a place of weeds and salt pits, a wasteland forever." In 2:12 the Lord continues, "You too, O Cushites, will be slain by my sword," and the prophet adds in 2:13, "He will stretch out his hand against the north and destroy Assyria, leaving Nineveh utterly desolate and dry as a desert." In 3:8, the Lord declares with a stinging finality, ""Therefore wait for me . . . for the day I will stand up to testify. I have decided to assemble the nations, to gather the kingdoms and to pour out my wrath on them—all my fierce anger. The whole world will be consumed by the fire of my jealous anger."

## Haggai

Haggai addresses the authority of the Lord and His power especially as the Lord Almighty speaks in 2:4-7: "Be strong, all you people of the land . . . and work. For I am with you . . . This is what I covenanted with you when you came out of Egypt. And my Spirit remains among you . . . In a little while I will once more shake the heavens and the earth . . . I will shake all nations . . . and I will fill this house with glory." He continues in 2:8-9: "The silver is mine and the gold is mine . . . the glory of this present house will be greater than the glory of the former house . . . And in this place I will grant peace." 2:21-22 then reiterates: "I will shake the heavens and the earth. I will overturn royal thrones and shatter the power of the foreign kingdoms; I will overthrow chariots and their drivers; horses and their riders will fall, each by the sword of his brother."

## Zechariah

Zechariah's prophecy is filled with indication of both the authority and power of the Lord as the Lord speaks of the judgment He brings upon His people as well as their deliverance, and as he also announces judgment against the nations. So in 1:3-4, the Lord Almighty declares, "Return to me . . . and I will return to you . . . Do not be like your forefathers, to whom the earlier prophets proclaimed: This is what the Lord Almighty says . . . Where are your forefathers now? . . . But did not my words and my decrees, which I commanded my servants the prophets, overtake your forefathers?" This note of authority and power so far as God's own people are concerned continues significantly in chapter 7. There Zechariah says in 7: 12, "They made their hearts as hard as flint and would not listen to the law or to the words that the Lord Almighty had sent by his Spirit through the earlier prophets. So the Lord Almighty was very angry." Zechariah continues in 7:13-14: "When I called, they did not listen; so when they called, I would not listen . . . I scattered them with a whirlwind among all the nations, where they were strangers. The land was left so desolate behind them that no one could come or go. This is how they made the pleasant land desolate."

In conclusion, Zechariah's mingling of the authority and power of the Lord is also evident in the Lord's assurance of salvation for His people, particularly as seen in chapter 8: "This is what the Lord Almighty says: 'I am very jealous for Zion; I am burning with jealousy for her . . . I will return to

Zion and dwell in Jerusalem. Then Jerusalem will be called the City of Truth, and the mountain of the Lord Almighty will be called the Holy Mountain ... I will bring them back to live in Jerusalem; they will be my people, and I will be faithful and righteous to them as their God"' (8:1-8).

# Chapter 11

# The Old Testament — Authority and Power in God's Mighty Acts

## The Writings

The books of the Old Testament that are sometimes referred to as "Writings" include Psalms, Proverbs, Ecclesiastes, Song of Solomon, Ezra, Nehemiah, Esther, Ruth, Daniel, Lamentations, and 1 and 2 Chronicles. In the opening chapter of this work we observed how God's authority and the powerful acts of God are brought to focus in two of Daniel's narratives, and later in the Psalms, we saw how the authority of God is affirmed by the power of God in creation. In this chapter we call attention to several other passages in the Writings which associate the authority of God with His powerful acts beyond creation.

## 1 Chronicles

Like 2 Samuel 6, 1 Chronicles 13 records the death of Uzzah who touched the ark of God which David was having transported to Jerusalem. 1 Chronicles 13:10 says, "The Lord's anger burned against Uzzah, and he struck him down because he had put his hand on the ark. So he died there before God." God's authority is apparent in the response of David to this demonstration of power according to 13:12-14: "David was afraid of God that day and asked, 'How can I ever bring the ark of God to me?' He did not take the ark to be with him in the City of David [but] took it aside to the house of Obed-Edom [whose house] the Lord blessed . . . and everything he had."

In 1 Chronicles 17 we find David affirming God's authority as David responds both to the Lord's intention to build a house/temple through his posterity and to David's own success. Thus in 17:16 David says, "Who am I, O Lord God, and what is my family that you have brought me this far?" David marvels in 17:19 that God "has done this great thing and made known all these great promises." He extols the Lord's authority in 17:20: "There is no one like you, O Lord, and there is no God but you, as we have heard with our own ears." Then David continues in 17:21 to marvel at the Lord's power: "And who is like your people Israel—the one nation on earth whose God went out to redeem a people for himself, and to make a name for yourself, and to perform great and awesome wonders by driving out nations from before your people, whom you redeemed from Egypt."

David's prayer in anticipation of the building of the temple is recorded in 1 Chronicles 29, and this prayer associates the authority and power of God. David acknowledges God's authority in 29:10-13: "Praise be to you, O Lord, God of our father Israel, from everlasting to everlasting . . . Yours, O Lord, is the kingdom; you are exalted as head over all . . . Now, our God, we give you thanks, and praise your glorious name." In these same verses David speaks of God's power: "Yours, O Lord, is the greatness and the power and the glory and the majesty and the splendor . . . In your hands are strength and power to exalt and give strength to all."

## 2 Chronicles

Solomon's prayer of dedication for the completed temple is found in 2 Chronicles 6. As Solomon knelt down and spread his hands toward heaven, 6:14 says that he prayed, "O Lord, God of Israel, there is no God like you in heaven or on earth," while according to 6:18, he said, "The heavens, even the highest heavens, cannot contain you. How much less this temple I have built." This recognition of divine authority is combined with recognition of the Lord's power working in various ways, as 6:24-25 says: "When your people Israel have been defeated by an enemy because they have sinned against you and when they turn back and confess your name . . . then hear from heaven and forgive the sin of your people Israel and bring them back to the land you gave them and their fathers." So also 6:26-27 says, "When the heavens are shut up and there is no rain . . . then hear from heaven and forgive the sin of your servants, your people Israel . . . and send rain on the land you gave your people for an inheritance." 6:28-31 mentions "famine or plague . . . or blight or mildew, locusts or grasshoppers . . . enemies . . . disaster . . . disease," and asks that the Lord hear the prayers and pleas of the people, even "each man according to all he does." The result is that "they will fear you and walk in your ways all the time they live in the land you gave the fathers." In 6:32-33, Solomon even asks that foreigners who "come [to pray] from a distant land because of your [God's] great name and your mighty hand and your outstretched arm," may find such a divine response that "all the peoples of the earth may know your name and fear you, as do your own people Israel, and may know that this house I have built bears your Name."

When Solomon finished his prayer, according to 2 Chronicles 7:1 the power of God was manifest as "fire came down from heaven and consumed the burnt offering and the sacrifices, and the glory of the Lord filled the temple." The result, according to 7:2-3, was that the priests could not enter the temple because of the glory of the Lord, and the Israelites, seeing the fire and the glory, acknowledged the authority of the Lord by kneeling "on the pavement with their faces to the ground, and they worshiped and gave thanks to the Lord, saying, 'He is good; his love endures forever.'"

2 Chronicles 7:8-10 records the week-long festival which took place in conjunction with the temple dedication, and there follows in 7:11-22 the well-known message of the Lord to Solomon when the Lord appeared to the king at night. In His message, the Lord warned that His power might be manifest in the shutting up of the heavens "so that there is no rain," or in the devouring of the land by locusts, and in the sending of "a plague among my people." But the people could respond to the Lord's authority if they would "humble themselves and pray and seek my face and turn from their wicked ways," with the result that the Lord "will hear from heaven and will forgive their sin and will heal their land."

In this same passage the Lord also warned about what would happen if the people rejected the authority of the Lord by turning away and forsaking "the decrees and commands I have given you and [going off] to serve other gods and worship them." His power would then be evident in punishment: "I will uproot Israel from my land, which I have given them, and will reject this temple I have consecrated for my Name. I will make it a byword and an object of ridicule among all peoples." When people ask why such a calamity has come upon the land of Israel and its temple, the answer will be found in the forsaking of authority: "Because they have forsaken the Lord, the God of their fathers, who brought them out of Egypt, and have embraced other gods, worshiping and serving them—that is why he brought all this disaster on them."

Respect for the authority of the Lord in response to the Lord's power is also apparent in Israel's dealings with the Egyptian king Shishak as recounted in 2 Chronicles 12. According to 12:5-8, after Rehoboam abandoned the law of the Lord, the Lord said to Rehoboam through the prophet Shemaiah, "You have abandoned me; therefore, I now abandon you to Shishak." Rehoboam and his leaders then humbled themselves and said "The Lord is just," to which the Lord replied, "My wrath will not be poured out on Jerusalem . . . They will, however, become subject to him [Shishak], so that they may learn the difference between serving me and serving the kings of other lands." Then after Shishak had plundered the temple, 12:12 says that when "Rehoboam humbled himself, the Lord's anger turned from him, and he was not totally destroyed. Indeed, there was some good in Judah."

A very pointed recognition of the authority and power of the Lord is found in 2 Chronicles 14:9-15, as Judah and its king Asa were confronted by the imposing force of the Cushites/Ethiopians. Asa called on God and said, "Lord, there is no one like you to help the powerless against the mighty.

Help us, O Lord our God, for we rely on you, and in your name we have come against this vast army. O Lord, you are our God; do not let man prevail against you." In the ensuing encounter, we are told of God's power, that "the Lord struck down the Cushites before Asa and Judah . . . Such a great number of Cushites fell that they could not recover; they were crushed before the Lord and his forces."

2 Chronicles 20 is concerned especially with the fortunes of Judah during the reign of Jehoshaphat as Judah faced attack from the Moabites and Ammonites, and the authority-power connection is prominent in this chapter. In his prayer (2 Chronicles 20:5-12), the king says, "O Lord, God of our fathers, are you not the God who is in heaven? You rule over all the kingdoms of the nations. Power and might are in your hand, and no one can withstand you." Recognition of God's power comes even more pointedly: "O our God, did you not drive out the inhabitants of this land before your people Israel and give it forever to the descendants of Abraham your friend?" And the prayer continues to acknowledge both God's power and authority: "If calamity comes upon us, whether the sword of judgment, or plague or famine, we will stand in your presence before this temple that bears your Name and will cry out to you in our distress, and you will hear us and save us."

In the same chapter 20, Jahaziel, a Levite, spoke for the Lord to the king and the residents of Judah and Jerusalem: "Do not be afraid or discouraged because of this vast army. For the battle is not yours, but God's . . . stand firm and see the deliverance the Lord will give you, O Judah and Jerusalem. Do not be afraid; do not be discouraged. Go out to face them tomorrow, and the Lord will be with you." In response to this assurance of power, the text says that "Jehoshaphat bowed with his face to the ground, and all the people of Judah and Jerusalem fell down in worship before the Lord . . . some Levites . . . stood up and praised the Lord, the God of Israel, with very loud voice." When victory had been achieved, 20:29 says, "The fear of God came upon all the kingdoms of the countries when they heard how the Lord had fought against the enemies of Israel."

2 Chronicles 32 recounts the threatened invasion of Judah and Jerusalem by the Assyrian king Sennacherib. There is much in this chapter that speaks to God's authority and power. According to 32:6-8, King Hezekiah of Judah encouraged his military leaders with these words: "Be strong and courageous. Do no be afraid or discouraged because of the king of Assyria and the vast army with him, for there is a greater power with us than with him. With him is only the arm of flesh, but with us is the Lord our God to help us and to fight our battles." In a message (32:10-15) to Hezekiah, Sennacherib denigrated the Lord's authority and power, and asked, "Who of all the gods of these nations that my fathers destroyed has been able to save his people from me? How then can your god deliver you from my hand?" Sennacherib reiterated this theme in subsequent letters, and his officers repeated them vocally to the people of Jerusalem, so that 32:19 says, "They spoke about the God of Jerusalem as they did about the gods of the other

peoples of the world—the work of men's hands." After Hezekiah and the prophet Isaiah cried out in prayer, 32:20 says, "The Lord sent an angel, who annihilated all the fighting men and the leaders and officers in the camp of the Assyrian king," with the result that Sennacherib "withdrew to his own land in disgrace . . . went into the temple of his god, [and] some of his sons cut him down with the sword." After this demonstration of God's power, 32:22-23 says that "the Lord saved Hezekiah and the people of Jerusalem from the hand of Sennacherib . . . and from the hand of all others," and respect for the Lord's authority ensued as "many brought offerings to Jerusalem for the Lord and valuable gifts for Hezekiah king of Judah."

Manasseh's reign in Jerusalem is addressed in 2 Chronicles 33. God's power was unleashed against Manasseh and his people because of their evil and rebellion. According to 33:11, "The Lord brought against them the army commanders of the king of Assyria, who took Manasseh prisoner, put a hook in his nose, bound him with bronze shackles, and took him to Babylon." The result was a change of heart for Manasseh who "sought the favor of the Lord his God and humbled himself greatly before the God of his fathers" (33:12). And when the Lord was moved by the plea of Manasseh, He "brought him back to Jerusalem and to his kingdom. Then Manasseh knew that the Lord is God" (33:13). Such recognition of the Lord's authority in the face of His power also led Manasseh to effect a kind of religious cleansing in Jerusalem, to the extent that "he got rid of the foreign gods and removed the image from the temple of the Lord, as well as all the altars he had built on the temple hill and in Jerusalem . . . Then he restored the altar of the Lord . . . and told Judah to serve the Lord, the God Israel," and although the people continued to sacrifice at their high places, they did so "only to the Lord their God" (33:15-17).

## Psalms

There are far too many psalms which demonstrate the authority-power connection for us to address them all here. But some are especially exemplary.

Consider Psalm 9 which begins in verse 1 with this recognition of authority, "I will praise you, O Lord, with all my heart; I will tell of all your wonders. I will be glad and rejoice in you; I will sing praise to your name, O Most High," and goes on in verse 7 to say, "The Lord reigns forever; he has established his throne for judgment," and adds in verse 11, "Sing praises to the Lord, enthroned in Zion; proclaim among the nations what he has done." This recognition of authority comes because of the Lord's power: "My enemies turn back; they stumble and perish before you" (11:3); "You have rebuked the nations and destroyed the wicked; you have blotted out their name for ever and ever . . . Endless ruin has overtaken the enemy, you have uprooted their cities; even the memory of them has perished" (11:5-6). And so it continues through the remainder of the psalm.

Psalm 18 also shows the connection between authority and power. The authority of the Lord is affirmed in a number of verses: "The Lord is my rock, my fortress and my deliverer . . . I call to the Lord, who is worthy of praise" (18:2-3); and, "For who is God besides the Lord? And who is the Rock except our God?" (18:31); and, "The Lord lives! Praise be to my Rock! Exalted be God my Savior!" (18:46). This testimony to authority flows from the power which the psalmist recognizes throughout the psalm: "In my distress I called to the Lord; I cried to my God for help. From his temple he heard my voice; my cry came before him, into his ears" (18:6); "He reached down from on high and took hold of me; he drew me out of deep waters. He rescued me from my powerful enemy, from my foes, who were too strong for me" (18:16-17). And 18:39-42 continues, "You armed me with strength for battle; you made my adversaries bow at my feet. You made my enemies turn their backs in flight, and I destroyed my foes . . . I beat them as fine as dust borne on the wind; I poured them out like mud in the streets."

In Psalm 40, the psalmist gives varied recognition to the Lord's authority. 40:3 says, "He put a new song in my mouth, a hymn of praise to our God. Many will see and fear, and put their trust in the Lord." 40:8 says, "I desire to do your will, O my God; your law is within my heart." And in 40:16-17, the psalmist writes, "May all who seek you rejoice and be glad in you; may those who love your salvation always say, 'The Lord be exalted!' . . . You are my help and my deliverer." The power of the Lord is recognized especially in 40:5: "Many, O Lord my God, are the wonders you have done. The things you have planned for us no one can recount to you; were I to speak and tell of them, they would be too many to declare."

Psalm 47 presents a very succinct indication of God's authority and power. Verses 1-2 say, "Clap your hands, all you nations; shout to God with cries of joy. How awesome is the Lord Most High, the great King over all the earth!" Verses 5-9 continue this exaltation: "God has ascended amid shouts of joy, the Lord amid the sounding of trumpets . . . Sing praises to God . . . sing praises to our King . . . For God is the King of all the earth . . . God reigns over the nations; God is seated on his holy throne . . . for the kings of the earth belong to God; he is greatly exalted." And what of the power of God? Verse 3 says, "He subdued nations under us, peoples under our feet. He chose our inheritance for us, the pride of Jacob, whom he loved."

Psalm 65 begins by exalting the Lord's authority in verses 1-3: "Praise awaits you, O God, in Zion; to you our vows will be fulfilled. O you who hear prayer, to you all men will come. When we were overwhelmed by sins, you forgave our transgressions." Then verses 5-7 continue by opening an exaltation of the power of God which continues through the rest of the psalm: "You answer us with awesome deeds of righteousness, O God our Savior . . . who formed the mountains by your power . . . who stilled the roaring of the seas, the roaring of their waves, and the turmoil of the nations."

Psalm 66 is much the same, beginning with acknowledgment of the Lord's authority in verses 1-2, "Shout with joy to God, all the earth! Sing the glory of his name; make his praise glorious," and continuing in verse 4, "All the earth bows down to you; they sing praise to you, they sing praise to your name." As to the power of God, verse 3 says, "Say to God, 'How awesome are your deeds! So great is your power that your enemies cringe before you.'" Verses 5-7 continue: "Come and see what God has done, how awesome his works in man's behalf! He turned the sea into dry land... He rules forever by his power, his eyes watch the nations—let not the rebellious rise up against him."

Psalm 68 also exalts the Lord's authority: "May God arise, may his enemies be scattered; may his foes flee before him" (68:1); "Sing to God, sing praise to his name, extol him who rides on the clouds—his name is the Lord—and rejoice before him" (68:4). The power of God is spoken of variously: "When you went out before your people, O God, when you marched through the wasteland, the earth shook, the heavens poured down rain" (68:7); "Kings and armies flee in haste" (68:12); "When the Almighty scattered the kings in the land, it was like snow fallen in Zalmon" (68:14); "Surely God will crush the heads of his enemies" (68:21); "Summon your power, O God; show us your strength, O God, as you have done before" (68:28).

Psalm 76 recognizes the authority of God from verse 1, "In Judah God is known; his name is great in Israel," to verse 12, "He breaks the spirit of rulers; he is feared by the kings of the earth." God's power is behind such respect: "There he broke the flashing arrows, the shields and swords, the weapons of war" (76:3); "Valiant men lie plundered, they sleep their last sleep; not one of the warriors can lift his hands. At your rebuke, O God of Jacob, both horse and chariot lie still" (76:5-6); "Surely your wrath against men brings you praise, and the survivors of your wrath are restrained" (76:10).

The lengthy Psalm 78 is based upon the demonstration of God's power in regard to the events of Israel's exodus period as well as Israel's failure to live faithfully in response to the Lord's authority. So the psalmist feels constrained to speak those "things from of old," which means "the praiseworthy deeds of the Lord, his power, and the wonders he has done" (78:2-4). At times Israel "remembered that God was their Rock, that God Most High was their Redeemer" (78:35), but His authority was constantly in question: "But they put God to the test and rebelled against the Most High; they did not keep his statutes" (78:56).

Psalm 105, also historically oriented, begins in verses 1-5 with a call to recognition of God's authority: "Give thanks to the Lord, call on his name... Sing to him, sing praise to him... Glory in his holy name... Look to the Lord and his strength" In these same verses, thanks are due because of "what he has done," while singing is to "tell of his wonderful acts," and the directive is to "remember the wonders he has done, his miracles, and the judgments he pronounced." The psalm then proceeds with extensive recognition of God's powerful acts especially in conjunction with the exodus tradition, and ends in verses 43-45 with this appropriate conclusion: "He brought out his people with rejoicing, his chosen ones with shouts of joy; he gave them the lands of the nations, and they fell heir to what others had toiled for—that they might keep his precepts and observe his laws."

Psalm 106 is a historical psalm like 105 and also with emphasis upon Israel's exodus tradition, although focusing primarily upon Israel's failures and rebellious acts. The psalm begins and ends with recognition of God's authority: "Praise the Lord. Give thanks to the Lord, for he is good; his love endures forever. Who can proclaim the mighty acts of the Lord or fully declare his praise?" (106:1-2); "Save us, O Lord our God, and gather us from the nations, that we may give thanks to your holy name and glory in your praise. Praise be to the Lord, the God of Israel, from everlasting to everlasting" (106:47-48). Israel's rebellion against the background of God's mighty acts permeates the psalm. Thus 106:7-8 says, "When our fathers were in Egypt, they gave no thought to your miracles; they did not remember your many kindnesses, and they rebelled by the sea, the Red Sea. Yet he saved them for his name's sake, to make his mighty power known."

We also see the association of authority and power in Psalm 135. The psalm begins with this recognition of divine authority: "Praise the Lord. Praise the name of the Lord; praise him, you servants of the Lord, you who minister in the house of the Lord, in the courts of the house of our God . . . I know that the Lord is great, that our Lord is greater than all gods" (135:1-5). Indication of divine power follows straightforward in 135:6-10: "The Lord does whatever pleases him, in the heavens and on the earth, in the seas and all their depths. He makes clouds rise from the ends of the earth; he sends lightning with the rain and brings out the wind from his storehouses. He struck down the firstborn of Egypt . . . He sent his signs and wonders into your midst, O Egypt . . . He struck down many nations and killed mighty kings."

Finally, we find the authority and power of God woven together in close context in Psalm 145. The authority of the Lord surfaces variously: "I will exalt you, my God the King; I will praise your name for ever and ever" (145:1); "Great is the Lord and most worthy of praise; his greatness no one can fathom" (145:3); "Your kingdom is an everlasting kingdom, and your dominion endures through all generations" (145:13); and in 145:21: "My mouth will speak in praise of the Lord. Let every creature praise his holy name for ever and ever." The power of God also surfaces variously, as in 145:4, "One generation will commend your works to another; and will tell of your mighty acts," or 145:5, "They will speak of the glorious splendor of your majesty, and I will meditate on your wonderful works." 145:6 adds, "They will tell of the power of your awesome works, and I will proclaim your great deeds," while 145:11-12 says, "They will . . . speak of your might, so that all men may know of your mighty acts." 145:16 continues, "You open your hand and satisfy the desires of every living thing," and 145:19 says, "He fulfills the desires of those who fear him; he hears their cry and saves them."

## Lamentations

Throughout Lamentations there is an almost constant weaving together of the themes of authority and power. So chapter 2 begins, "How the Lord has covered the Daughter of Zion with the cloud of his anger!" 2:5 says, "The Lord is like an enemy; he has swallowed up Israel," and 2:18 adds, "The hearts of the people cry out to the Lord," while 2:20 insists, "Look, O Lord, and consider: Whom have you ever treated like this?" This tone of authority is set against the reality of Israel's punishment which displayed the Lord's power. Thus 2:2 says, "Without pity the Lord has swallowed up all the dwellings of Jacob; in his wrath he has torn down the strongholds of the Daughter of Judah. He has brought her kingdom and its princes down to the ground in dishonor." In 2:6 we find: "The Lord has made Zion forget her appointed feasts and her Sabbaths; in his fierce anger he has spurned both king and priest." And 2:8-9 continues to lament the Lord's punishing power: "The Lord determined to tear down the wall around the Daughter of Zion ... He made ramparts and walls lament; together they wasted away ... Her king and her princes are exiled among the nations, the law is no more, and her prophets no longer find visions from the Lord." With great frankness, 2:17 says, "The Lord has done what he planned; he has fulfilled his word, which he decreed long ago. He has overthrown you without pity, he has let the enemy gloat over you, he has exalted the horn of your foes."

Lamentations continues in this way, recognizing the power of God as in 4:11, "The Lord has given full vent to his wrath; he has poured out his fierce anger. He kindled a fire in Zion that consumed her foundations." And the lament concludes in 5:19-22 with this clear recognition of divine authority: "You, O Lord, reign forever; your throne endures from generation to generation ... Restore us to yourself, O Lord, that we may return ... unless you have utterly rejected us and are angry with us beyond measure."

# Chapter 12

# Authority and Power in Question

## Power Expects Authority

The survey we have just completed shows how important the themes of authority and power are to biblical revelation. In both the Old Testament and the New Testament, divine authority is affirmed again and again. Such affirmation of authority often comes by appeal to or demonstration of divine power. Divine power is in evidence in creation and the natural world as well as specific historical acts, and in the New Testament it is principally Jesus through whom those acts occur, thus affirming His own divine authority.

It seems rather obvious that power is expected to lead to affirmation of authority. The demonstrations of power accomplished by Moses and Aaron in the presence of Pharaoh had that goal. And when Jesus responded to John the Baptist's question (Matthew 11:2-3; cf. Luke 7:18-19) about Jesus' messianic authority ("Are you the one who was to come, or should we expect someone else?"), His response came basically as "look at the power" kind of evidence: "the blind receive sight, the lame walk, those who have leprosy are cured, the deaf hear, the dead are raised, and the good news is preached to the poor" (Matthew 11:5; cf. Luke 7:22). These miracles or acts of power were expected to help the Baptist appreciate and affirm the authority of Jesus.

## Doubts

For whatever reasons, demonstrations of power, even miracles, do not always persuade people about divine authority. The plagues in Egypt did not persuade Pharaoh, albeit for a time, and in the end, the biblical account indicates that nothing would persuade him even unto his own death. John the Baptist, on the other hand, was apparently persuaded although we have no direct confirmation. What we do know is that from biblical days, either Old Testament or New Testament, God's power, displayed either in the wonders of creation or in mighty acts, be they miracles or signs or works, has not always persuaded people about God's authority or for that matter about Jesus' authority.

John 6 shows this very clearly. According to 6:26, Jesus said, "I tell you the truth, you are looking for me, not because you saw miraculous signs but because you ate the loaves and had your fill." If the signs would have had their intended effect, then the work of God would have been done in those who saw them, as Jesus said in 6:29: "The work of God is this: to believe in the one he has sent." For many there was no faith. So 6:30 indicates that they wanted more signs or something that would convince them: "What miraculous sign then will you give that we may see it and believe you? What will you do?" And Jesus, in His response, made clear what He expected, as 6:36 says: "But as I told you, you have seen me and still you do not believe." So for some people, seeing the signs, and even seeing Jesus perform the signs, was not enough to produce faith.

This is an ongoing reality. There is only so much that can be done to persuade people about the truth. The words of Jesus may have that effect by themselves. But power is available to back up the words, as Jesus says in John 10:38: "Even though you do not believe me, believe the miracles, that you may know and understand that the Father is in me, and I in the Father." For the disciples, at least, the desired effect was achieved, as Peter said in John 6:69: "We believe and know that you are the holy One of God." But for many such is not the case.

Since the period of the early church, doubts about the manifest power of God have continued. In the face of biblical miracles that are said to demonstrate and defend the authority of God and His Son Jesus Christ, many have denied that such miracles ever took place. The result of such denial has always been an erosion of the perceived or believed authority of God and of Jesus. And with that erosion of faith has come an almost certain denial of the supernatural realm.

By the end of the nineteenth century, this denial of the demonstrable power of God was seen in the increasing denial of biblical miracles. The miracles and signs that the Bible indicates were designed to demonstrate the authority of God and of Jesus were not only being denied but were consequently regarded as being unable to demonstrate such authority. Indeed, biblical miracles that in any way suggested the existence of a supernatural realm were being laid aside, and supernatural claims of any kind, from the Bible or elsewhere, were also being called into question. Here we give only brief attention to such questioning.

## David Hume

One name often associated with a negative view of miracles and thus of biblical miracles is David Hume, the Scottish philosopher/historian who lived from 1711 to 1776. In the 10th section ("Of Miracles") of his work, *An Enquiry concerning Human Understanding*[6], 1777 edition, Hume expressed a view which has become a stepping stone for many to follow in their own approach to the subject or question of miracles.

Hume did not deny absolutely that miracles, even biblical miracles, occurred. At the close of section 10 he says, "We may conclude that the Christian religion not only was at first attended with miracles, but even at this day cannot be believed by any reasonable person without one." He explains further, "Mere reason is insufficient to convince us of its veracity. And whoever is moved by *faith* to assent to it is conscious of a continued miracle in his own person, which subverts all the principles of his understanding and gives him a determination to believe what is most contrary to custom and experience."

Hume's essay is really oriented toward miracles "in general," and he only touches upon biblical miracles. He has the same skepticism about biblical miracles that he does about miracles "in general." This skepticism arises especially from the nature of experience, and miracles are obviously not part of typical human experience. Hume says, "The reason why we place any credit in witnesses and historians is not derived from any *connection* which we perceive a priori between testimony and reality, but because we are accustomed to find a conformity between them." He continues, "But when the fact attested is such a one as has seldom fallen under our observation, here is a contest of two opposite experiences, of which the one destroys the other as far as its force goes, and the superior can only operate on the mind by the force which remains."

Not only does experience teach us that miracles don't happen, Hume says, but when claims about miracles have been made, they have tended to occur when new religions were being established. They happened among people who were not the most intellectually astute, or more precisely, "they are observed chiefly to abound among ignorant and barbarous nations." Then too it has often been shown that many miraculous claims have been false claims. He says, "The many instances of forged miracles and prophecies and supernatural events, which, in all ages, have either been detected by contrary evidence or which detect themselves by their absurdity, prove sufficiently the strong propensity of mankind to the extraordinary and marvelous, and ought reasonably to beget a suspicion against all relations of this kind."

Thus if there is full evidence, there is no miracle: "There never was a miraculous event established [in any history] on so full an evidence." He adds, "There is not to be found, in all history, any miracle attested by a sufficient number of men of such unquestioned good sense, education, and learning as to secure us against all delusion in themselves." Such men would also be "of such undoubted integrity as to place them beyond all suspicion of any design to deceive others," they would be "of such credit and reputation in the eyes of mankind as to have a great deal to lose in case of their being detected in any falsehood," and they would have to attest facts "in such a public manner and in so celebrated a part of the world as to render the detection [of falsehood] unavoidable—all which circumstances are requisite to give us a full assurance in the testimony of men."

Finally we may note that Hume warns about trying to understand biblical miracles (and he has the miracles of the Pentateuch specifically in mind) from the perspective of reason and not from faith. He says that his approach to miracles "may serve to confound those dangerous friends or disguised enemies to the Christian religion who have undertaken to defend it by the principles of human reason." He asserts that "our most holy religion is founded on *faith*, not on reason; and it is a sure method of exposing it to put it to such a trial as it is by no means fitted to endure."

So it is that one concludes that whatever miracles Hume concedes to the Bible, he concedes on the basis of faith. We might say that faith allows miracles, or that faith comes first and then miracles. But the biblical persuasion is often the other way around. It is the miracles that lead to faith. It was the healing of the paralyzed man at Capernaum that led to faith or knowledge, and the purpose of John's Gospel points to the same conclusion. Signs or miracles happen so that people may believe.

## Ernest Renan

One biblical scholar who seems to have followed Hume's line of thought almost to the point of having Hume's work before him was the French scholar Ernest Renan who lived from 1823 to 1892. His book *Life of Jesus/Vie de Jésus*, first published in 1863, shows clearly how Renan approached the supernatural and miracles. In his Introduction[7], he says that the historian, especially the one working with the four basic Gospels, "needs to be very cautious—to examine the texts, and to proceed carefully by induction." And he says, "There is one class of narratives especially, to which this principle must necessarily be applied. Such are narratives of supernatural events."

Thus the miracles are particularly suspect: "None of the miracles with which the old histories are filled took place under scientific conditions." He continues, "Observation, which has never once been falsified, teaches us that miracles never happen but in times and countries in which they are believed, and before persons disposed to believe them." If the miracle could be tested, that would be fine, but "no miracle ever occurred in the presence of men capable of testing its miraculous character. Neither common people nor men of the world are able to do this. It requires great precautions and long habits of scientific research."

Renan does not say that miracles are impossible, but "up to this time a miracle has never been proved." He says that if a miracle worker, a "thaumaturgus," were to claim to raise the dead, the manner of substantiating his claim would follow a certain process: "A commission, composed of physiologists, physicists, chemists, persons accustomed to historical criticism, would be named. This commission would choose a corpse, would assure itself that the death was real, would select the room in which the experiment should be made, would arrange the whole system of precautions, so as to leave no chance of doubt." He adds that if a resurrection were accomplished under these conditions, "a probability almost equal to certainty would be established."

That's not all, because it should be possible to repeat the experiment under a variety of circumstances which should not pose a particular problem for the miracle worker/thaumaturgus. If the miracle could be successfully repeated, two things would be proved: "First, that supernatural events happen in the world; second, that the power of producing them belongs or is delegated to, certain persons." Obviously for Renan, the problem is that no miracle ever occurs under these kinds of circumstances: "Always hitherto the thaumaturgus has chosen the subject of the experiment, chosen the spot, chosen the public." So Renan provides a logical conclusion to his method: "Until a new order of things prevails, we shall maintain then this principle of historical criticism – that a supernatural account cannot be admitted as such, that it always implies credulity or imposture, that the duty of the historian is to explain it, and seek to ascertain what share of truth or of error it may conceal." And for his work on Jesus, these are "the rules which have been followed in the composition of this work."

It seems rather obvious that Renan was looking for something that would not be a miracle, but would be ordinary, something occurring or possible to occur again and again. Even if it was just for the purpose of some kind of scientific proof, the sheer possibility of repetition he wants seems foreign to the very nature of what is called a miracle. Miracles, and certainly particular miracles, are not a matter for repetition and examination but for wonder and awe. There is no more assurance that any act repeated under a variety of conditions, as Renan calls for, would be more likely treated as a miracle than is already the case with so-called miracles, and certainly the biblical miracles. If miracles become ordinary matters, repeated again and again, are they still miracles, and not ordinary occurrences? Would they lead to faith as the biblical miracles seem designed to lead us?

## Albert Schweitzer's Review

Early in the twentieth century, Albert Schweitzer (1875-1965) wrote *The Quest of the Historical Jesus* (German title *Geschichte der Leben-Jesu-Forschung*) which was first published in 1906.[8] In reviewing the books known as "lives of Jesus" which had been written to his time, Schweitzer made some pertinent (for our purposes) comments about miracles.

Of the work by Herman Samuel Reimarus[9] (1694-1768), Schweitzer notes that for Reimarus it was "useless to appeal to miracles . . . as evidence of the founding of a new religion" because miracle accounts are much affected by tradition. But Reimarus acknowledged that "Jesus affected cures which in the eyes of his contemporaries were miraculous . . . Their purpose was to prove him to be the Messiah. He forbade these miracles to be made known 'with the sole purpose of making people more curious about them.'" Other miracles "have no basis in fact," but are placed in the narrative because of "the feeling that the miracle stories of the Old Testament must be repeated in the case of Jesus, but on a grander scale. He did no real miracles; otherwise, the demands for a sign would be incomprehensible . . . If only a single miracle had been publicly, convincingly, undeniably performed by Jesus before all the people . . . all the world would have come over to him." So Reimarus acknowledges that the function of miracles, real or not, was to substantiate the authority of Jesus, to prove that He was the Messiah.

As Schweitzer continues his survey, he observes that the real "battle over miracle had not yet begun. But miracle no longer plays a part of any importance; it is a firmly established principle that the teaching of Jesus, and religion in general, hold their place solely in virtue of their inner reasonableness, not by the support of external authentication." This of course flies in the face of the whole purpose of miracles or demonstrations of power as we have noted in the biblical record. It is such "external authentication" that is vitally important to the biblical writers.

Schweitzer continues and indicates that the lives of Jesus were increasingly controlled by rationalism, the persuasion that it was possible to subject the life of Jesus to what seemed reasonable so that various writers almost unwittingly made Jesus the product of their own reason. At many points the writers would not accept the Gospel record, but they thought they could actually tell what the record should be, at least as it seemed reasonable to them, so that they imposed themselves on Jesus. For miracles this meant that "all of them made it a principle to lose no opportunity of reducing the number of miracles; where they can explain a miracle by natural causes, they do not hesitate for a moment." Schweitzer continues, "But we do not yet find here the deliberate rejection of all miracles, the elimination of everything supernatural which intrudes itself into the life of Jesus . . . Earlier rationalism left a remnant of miracle: it depends on the degree of enlightenment in the individual whether the irreducible minimum of the supernatural is larger or smaller."

In assessing the work of Johan Jakob Hess[10] (1741 to 1828) so far as miracles are concerned, Schweitzer says, "Hess admits that miracles are a stumbling block. But they are part of the Gospel narrative and revelation; had Jesus been only a moral teacher and not the Son of God, they would not have been necessary." According to Schweitzer, Hess cautions that "we must be careful, however, not to prize miracles for their own sake, but to look primarily to their ethical teaching." It was "the mistake of the Jews to regard all the acts of Jesus solely from the point of view of their strange and miraculous character . . . whereas we, from distaste for miracle as such, run the risk of excluding from the Gospel events which are bound up with the Gospel." Hess held that the supernatural birth and the bodily resurrection of Jesus were essential miracles, and also held that the raising of Lazarus was authentic. Schweitzer notes that Hess "rationalized" the Gospel narrative whenever that was possible so that not only miracles but parables became "incomprehensible" and "barely recognizable." Such an approach "held its ground in theology for some sixty years and passed over into some dozen Lives of Jesus."

The work of Paulus[11] (Heinrich Eberhard Gottlob Paulus, 1761-1851) on the life of Christ was published in 1828, and Schweitzer refers to this as "fully developed rationalism." The "main interest centres in the explanations of the miracles." Paulus did not want his views of miracles to be "the principal thing." Then, very pointedly for our purpose, Schweitzer quotes Paulus: "How empty would devotion or religion be if one's spiritual well-being depended on whether one believed in miracles or not!" He also says, "The truly miraculous thing about Jesus is himself, the purity and serene holiness of his character, which is nevertheless genuinely human, and adapted to the imitation and emulation of mankind."

Here we see how the very point of a miracle such as the healing of the paralyzed man at Capernaum is brushed aside. It is the miracle, the power, which really told who Jesus was, which pointed to His divine authority. It is only through the miraculous that Jesus Himself was really known and appreciated. Jesus was revealing much more than the purity and holiness of His character. He was revealing His authority, authority that can come only from God and authority that points to divinity.

According to Schweitzer's perspective of Paulus, the question of miracles "does not really exist," or exists only for those who are under a delusion which does not really understand God. Thus, the only problem for "normal intelligence" is "to discover the secondary causes of the 'miracles' of Jesus." Schweitzer goes on to show what many of those secondary causes were for Paulus such as Jesus being taken for a ghost walking on the water when He was really walking along the shore in a mist. Schweitzer eventually says that this "consistently rationalistic" life of Jesus received much opposition, and added, "The method is doomed to failure because the author saves his own sincerity only at the expense of that of his characters. He makes the disciples of Jesus assume miracles where they could not possibly have seen them and makes Jesus himself allow miracles to be imagined where he must necessarily have protested against such a delusion."

Another of the notable works on the life of Jesus that Schweitzer reviews came from David Friedrich Strauss[12] (1808-1874) in 1835, although Strauss's views underwent considerable change over time in subsequent editions of his work. What made Strauss's work significant was his use of myth/legend to explain much of the supernatural in the biblical accounts of Jesus. He did not find it necessary to re-tell miracles in what seemed to be reasonable forms, but he could attribute mythical or legendary qualities to miracle accounts. Whatever happened had been overlaid with mythical features. Thus some of the healing miracles are regarded as historical, "but not in the form in which tradition has preserved them," says Schweitzer. Schweitzer also observes that Strauss put nature miracles under the heading "Sea Stories and Fish Stories" which contained a significant "admixture of the mythical."

Especially significant in this regard are miracles that have to do with Jesus Himself and His own history such as the transfiguration, the resurrection, and the ascension. These contain layers of myth or legend and any attempts to account for the different layers pose a dilemma. Schweitzer adds, "In reading Strauss's discussions one is hardly struck by their radical character, because of the admirable dialectical skill with which he shows the total impossibility of any explanation which does not take account of myth." The net result of Strauss's work was that it "put an end to miracle as a matter of historical belief, and gave mythological explanation its due." In some ways this was actually an advantage over what had been happening in that it left a more historical Jesus than had been true previously.

Finally, in considering Schweitzer's review, we note the work of Bruno Bauer[13] (1809 to 1882) who wrote not so much about the life of Jesus as he did about how to approach the sources, the Gospels, in order to study the life of Jesus. Of significance for our purposes, so far as Schweitzer explains it, is that Bauer stripped the Gospels of almost anything, including miracles, that might be considered historical. Bauer said, "Jesus . . . must perform these innumerable, these astounding miracles because, according to the view which the Gospels represent, he is the Messiah; he must perform them in order to prove himself to be the Messiah—and yet no one recognizes him as the Messiah! That is the greatest miracle of all, that the people had not long ago recognized the Messiah in this wonder-worker." How did the miracles come to be a part of the narrative? Schweitzer continues to quote Bauer: "Jesus could only be held to be the Messiah in consequence of doing miracles; he only began to do miracles when, in the faith of the early church, he rose from the dead as Messiah, and the facts that he rose as Messiah and that he did miracles are one and the same fact."

Schweitzer continues his assessment of Bauer by showing that Bauer regarded the Christian and biblical portrait of Jesus as one which "usurped the place of the true religion, and in this petrified form it holds prisoner all the real forces of religion." Miracles, then, "to which the Christian religion has always appealed, and to which it gives a quite fundamental importance, [are] the appropriate symbol of this false victory over the world." It follows then, that "not only miracle . . . but the portrait of Jesus Christ as drawn in the Gospels, is a stereotyping of that false idea of victory over the world.

The Christ of the Gospel history thought of as a really historical figure . . . would be a figure at which humanity would shudder, a figure which could only inspire dismay and horror."

The net result of Bauer's assessment of the biblical presentation of Jesus is one of virtual futility. Schweitzer says of Bauer, "The question which so much exercises people's minds – whether Jesus was the historical Christ – is answered in the sense that everything that the historical Christ is, everything that is said of him, everything that is known of him, belongs to the world of imagination . . . the imagination of the Christian community." Ultimately, Schweitzer says of Bauer's view, "The result is negative. There never was any historical Jesus."

We can say that Bauer was right, that Jesus had to perform miracles "in order to prove himself to be the Messiah." But Bauer was wrong to say that "no one recognize[d] him as the Messiah." Although not everyone did, the Gospels make it clear that some did. It has been that way ever since the New Testament period. Not everyone has responded positively to the miracles or power that the Bible says Jesus and others displayed. Not everyone has been moved by such power to accept or believe the authority of Jesus, that He was indeed the Christ or Messiah or Son of God. But some did, and many still do!

## Rudolf Bultmann

Schweitzer's work on the quest for the historical Jesus was written shortly after the beginning of the twentieth century. It was the German scholar Rudolf Bultmann (1884-1976) who probably more definitively than anyone else brought the results of what Schweitzer wrote about into the mainstream of the twentieth century. As far as miracles go, it is Bultmann's essay, "New Testament and Mythology,"[14] based on a lecture he delivered in 1941, which best summarizes what happened to the power, the miracles.

Bultmann gets right to the issue: "*Man's knowledge and mastery of the world* have advanced to such an extent through science and technology that it is no longer possible for anyone seriously to hold the New Testament view of the world—in fact, there is no one who does." He goes on to say, "We no longer believe in the three-storied universe which the creeds take for granted." And he adds, "There is no longer any heaven in the traditional sense of the word. The same applies to hell in the sense of a mythical underworld beneath our feet."[15]

It follows, then, that if the New Testament view of the world is laid aside, much else will be laid aside as well. So Bultmann says, "Now that the forces and the laws of nature have been discovered, we can no longer believe in *spirits, whether good or evil.*" Of miracles specifically, he says, "The miracles of the New Testament have ceased to be miraculous, and to defend their historicity by recourse to nervous disorders or hypnotic effects only serves to underline the fact." He continues to emphasize the effect of modern understanding: "It is impossible to use electric light and the wireless and to avail ourselves of modern medical and surgical discoveries, and at the same time to believe in the New Testament world of spirits and miracles."[16]

There are, of course, other aspects of biblical and New Testament content which come under Bultmann's scrutiny. For our purposes we note only what Bultmann says of the resurrection of Jesus: "The *resurrection of Jesus* is just as difficult for modern man, if it means an event whereby a living supernatural power is released which can henceforth be appropriated through the sacraments." Bultmann says that "to the biologist such language is meaningless," and that "the idealist would not object to the idea of a life immune from death, but he could not believe that such a life is made available by the resurrection of a dead person." That would involve a "nature miracle," and "apart from the incredibility of such a miracle . . . [one] cannot see how an event like this could be the act of God, or how it could affect his own life."[17]

Eventually then, Bultmann says of the resurrection that the New Testament "side by side with the historical event of the crucifixion . . . sets the definitely non-historical event of the resurrection." This is a "combination of myth and history" which "presents a number of difficulties" which Bultmann feels can be seen from "certain inconsistencies in the New Testament material."[18] He also acknowledges that "it cannot be denied that the resurrection of Jesus is often used in the New Testament as a miraculous proof." But "the resurrection narratives . . . are most certainly later embellishments of the primitive tradition . . . An historical fact which involves a resurrection from the dead is utterly inconceivable!"[19] And he adds, "If the event of Easter Day is in any sense an historical event additional to the event of the cross, it is nothing else than the rise of faith in the risen Lord . . . The resurrection itself is not an event of past history."[20]

More than seventy years have passed since Bultmann delivered his famous lecture. The most appropriate response we can make for our purposes in this book is to observe what is really quite obvious. In those seventy years the world has moved far beyond the science and technology of the early twentieth century. It is no longer simply a world of electric lights and the wireless, and of what were then modern medical and surgical discoveries. Now it is a world of space exploration, information technology, and biological minutiae such as DNA. Computers and wireless cell phones/devices of all kinds are common place and even their capabilities change almost daily. Laser and sonar surgery are common.

What of miracles and especially the biblical miracles, the biblical demonstrations of power, in the light of our now twenty-first century knowledge? It is safe to say that more people than ever in the world's history believe that biblical miracles are part of history, that they are not just events which were overlaid with mythical elements. The biblical miracles, even the resurrection of Jesus, are accepted as historical events by scientists, by doctors, by computer whizzes, by theologians and biblical scholars, and of course, by many people with ordinary talents and abilities.

To be sure, there are still many skeptics, and many who still agree with those who have previously written off biblical miracles from the realm of historical reality. However, many Christians not only accept the biblical miracles as historical, but they also attribute their own faith to biblical miracles. They have come to faith precisely in the manner of the purpose of John's Gospel. They have considered the miracles of the Bible and especially the miracles of Jesus, accepted them as signs pointing to divine authority and especially the divine or heavenly authority of Jesus, and they have become people of faith.

I have long made it a practice to say to my own students something like this. There are many people with Ph.D.'s from Harvard or M.I.T. or a host of other universities who do not believe that the biblical miracles really happened, or that Jesus performed the miracles that were recorded in the Gospels, or that Jesus rose from the dead. But there are some people with Ph.D.'s from Harvard or M.I.T. or a host of other universities who do believe that the biblical miracles really happened, that Jesus performed miracles, and that Jesus rose from the dead, literally and physically. For such believers the miracles are indeed signs that point to divine, heavenly authority. Obviously those who regard the biblical miracles and especially the miracles of Jesus as real historical events have a very high regard for divine authority and especially for the divine authority of Jesus.

## Affirmation—C. S. Lewis

For those who believe in biblical miracles and regard such miracles as historical events, there are many apologists, although none is more significant and popular for this position than C. S. Lewis. Lewis's book, *Miracles*[21], was published in 1947. Basic to his approach to the subject of miracles is the need to distinguish between naturalism and supernaturalism. Naturalism means "the doctrine that only Nature—the whole interlocked system—exists."[22] Lewis holds that just as many things exist now in what is not a natural state, so it is possible to believe that there is a supernatural reality, that which is not natural. Thus, he says, "There is, then, a God who is not a part of Nature."[23]

And, he adds, "To believe that Nature produced God, or even the human mind is ... absurd."[24]

It follows that "if you begin by ruling out the supernatural you will perceive no miracles. We must now add that you will equally perceive no miracles until you believe that nature works according to regular laws."[25] There have been many so-called miracles or incredible claims that were proven to be false. But miracles "are in a wholly different position. If there were fire-breathing dragons our big-game hunters would find them: but no one ever pretended that the Virgin Birth or Christ's walking on the water could be reckoned on to recur"[26] [although Hume and Renan might like that to happen for further investigation].  Miracles don't break the laws of nature.  From the standpoint of the scientist, a miracle is "a form of doctoring, tampering, (if you like) cheating. It introduces a new factor into the situation, namely supernatural force, which the scientist had not reckoned on."[27] But miracles do not break any laws. He says, "The laws at once take it over. Nature is ready." Thus, "A miracle is emphatically not an event without cause or without results. Its cause is the activity of God: its results follow according to Natural law."[28] So Lewis stresses that "the rightful demand that all reality should be consistent and systematic does not therefore exclude miracles." This demand "reminds us that miracles, if they occur, must, like all events, be revelations of the total harmony of all that exists." So it is that he says, "By definition, miracles must of course interrupt the usual course of Nature; but if they are real they must, in the very act of so doing, assert all the more the unity and self-consistency of total reality at some deeper level."[29]

In the Epilogue to his book, Lewis issues some cautions for those who approach the subject of miracles. He says, "When you turn from the New Testament to modern scholars, remember that you go among them as a sheep among wolves. Naturalistic assumptions, beggings of the question . . . will meet you on every side – even from the pens of clergymen." He admits, "We all have Naturalism in our bones and even conversion does not at once work the infection out of our system."[30] When using the books of those who are so infected, "you must therefore be continually on guard. You must develop a nose like a bloodhound for those steps in the argument which depend not on historical and linguistic knowledge but on the concealed assumption that miracles are impossible, improbable, or improper." Lewis continues by stressing that "you must really re-educate yourself: must work hard and consistently to eradicate from your mind the whole type of thought in which we have all been brought up."[31]

# Chapter 13

# The Biblical Response

The previous chapter showed how the biblical presentation of power, especially in the form of miracles, has undergone such questioning as to make the entire biblical record eventually somewhat power-less to some people. The pros and cons of biblical power and miracles are virtually without resolution in the minds of those who are on one side or the other of the question. Knowledgeable people deny biblical miracles, and knowledgeable people affirm such miracles. The weight of the vote or opinion doesn't resolve the differences.

Our purpose in this chapter is to consider how the biblical writers themselves respond or might respond to doubts or denials of what may be called the visible powers of God, miracles being the typical form of such powers. Here we limit consideration to the New Testament, since that is where this book gets its impetus, and since that is where power and authority are closely associated in consideration of the witness of Jesus Christ.

It is clear that the New Testament writers don't confront the questioning of power or miracles in the way that theologians and biblical students might do so today. Since the biblical writers themselves represented a view which supported divine power and demonstrations of the miraculous, especially in Jesus, they are not writing with a significant history of opposition to miracles in mind. In the biblical record, there is no extended questioning of miracles like we find in biblical scholarship of the post-Reformation era, and there is thus no need of an extended defense of biblical miracles as we find in C. S. Lewis. The biblical responses to such a subject are somewhat tempered, and yet there are some, among others, which merit consideration here.

## Denying the Power

The first consideration for our purposes is that found in the context of 2 Timothy 3. The chapter begins by warning about "terrible times in the last days" (3:1), and goes on to speak of people who are characterized by having, among other things, "a form of godliness but denying its power" (3:5). The word for power here is the familiar Greek word *dunamis* which, as we have seen, is often translated "miracle." There is nothing here except the word *dunamis*/miracle/power which would tie the intent of the passage directly to the subject of power or miracles as substantiation of authority, but there is nothing to deny such a connection. It might well be that Paul has in mind here the power that brings self-control, the kind of self-control that seems to be absent in "the last days," when people are "lovers of themselves, lovers of money, boastful, proud," etc. as the passage goes. Perhaps it is fitting to say that he speaks of the time when there will be no place for power at all, no place for power that produces morality, and no place for power that substantiates authority.

The passage in 2 Timothy 3 goes on to speak of those who are "always learning but never able to acknowledge the truth" (3:7). It then mentions the Egyptian magicians, Jannes and Jambres, the somewhat inept miracle workers who opposed Moses until their own power ran out. If the Egyptians learned that the power of God operating through Moses and Aaron was greater than the power operating through their magicians, they didn't necessarily show it in any clear or lasting response. Just as those who were present at the healing of the paralyzed man could not accept the authority of Jesus without the demonstration of power, so the form of religion that is power-denying cannot accept the evident truth. Indeed, there is no evidence that everyone who observed the paralyzed man healed by Jesus also believed that Jesus had authority from God to forgive sins.

Finally, the passage refers to the authority of Scripture (3:16) which is God-breathed and useful for the work of God. If the very Scripture which is thus useful is denied as to its miracles or demonstrations of power, how can its authority be maintained any more than the authority of those, like Jesus, whose demonstrations of power are recorded in Scripture? It can't! Thus the authority of Scripture itself has been broadly called into question or denied, and with such questioning of the authority of Scripture, questioning of the nature and authority of Jesus has followed.

1 John has a similar concern for the relationship between Jesus and "the Christ," and the coming of Jesus Christ "in the flesh." 1 John 2:21 says, "I do not write to you because you do not know the truth, but because you know it and because no lie comes from the truth." Then John continues in 2:22-23: "Who is the liar? It is the man who denies that Jesus is the Christ. Such a man is the antichrist—he denies the Father and the Son. No one who denies the Son has the Father; whoever acknowledges the Son has the Father also." 1 John 4:2-3 adds to this assessment: "This is how you can recognize the Spirit of God: Every spirit that acknowledges that Jesus Christ has come

in the flesh is from God, but every spirit that does not acknowledge Jesus is not from God. This is the spirit of the antichrist, which you have heard is coming and even now is already in the world." It is quite logical to expect that where the power of Jesus is denied, the authority of Jesus, meaning especially His divine authority and His special relationship to God, will be denied as well.

The direction that comes at the end of 2 Timothy 3:5 in regard to power-deniers is sobering: "Have nothing to do with them." How do we assess such a warning? We must remember that Paul has already given Timothy, God's "workman" as he calls him, much guidance in this regard in preceding verses in order that Timothy might be one "who does not need to be ashamed and who correctly handles the word of truth" (2:15). So it would be good to avoid such people as are mentioned in 3:1-5 if it means that Timothy would be compromised by association with them. It is to Timothy, not those "people," that Paul directs the words of 2:22: "Flee the evil desires of youth, and pursue righteousness, faith, love and peace, along with those who call on the Lord out of a pure heart."

Paul also warns Timothy in 2:23 not to "have anything to do with foolish and stupid arguments, because you know they produce quarrels." Why not be competitive and quarrelsome? Because the Lord's servant "must not quarrel; instead, he must be kind to everyone, able to teach, not resentful" (2:24). There is very clear reason for this: "Those who oppose him he must gently instruct, in the hope that God will grant them repentance leading them to a knowledge of the truth, and that they will come to their senses and escape from the trap of the devil, who has taken them captive to do his will" (2:25-26). There is a time and a place for ethical/moral confrontation and for theological debate, but in many cases it is best to avoid such confrontation, and even debate, if such confrontation and debate become little more than a quarrel.

## Resurrection and Reason

A second New Testament consideration in approaching the power or miracle debate is that found in 1 Corinthians 15. This significant chapter speaks extensively to the subject of resurrection, and develops a very logical approach to both the resurrection of Jesus and what might be called the general resurrection. Very simply, Paul says that Jesus rose from the dead and therefore we have reason to believe that all humanity awaits a general resurrection. Death has been conquered in Jesus. If Jesus didn't rise from the dead, then there is no reason to believe that there will be a general resurrection . . . death has not been conquered.

Paul proclaims a two-fold defense of the resurrection of Jesus. First there is the testimony of Scripture. He doesn't tell us what that Scripture is, but his appeal is quite clear. Jesus died and rose again on the third day, "according to the Scriptures" (15:3-4). Second, Paul appeals to eyewitness testimony. After His resurrection, Jesus "appeared to Peter . . . to the Twelve . .

. to more than five hundred of the brothers at the same time . . . to James . . . to all the apostles . . . to me [Paul] also" (15:5-8).

It is the logic of Paul's position that is especially important. He says, "If it is preached that Christ has been raised from the dead, how can some of you say that there is no resurrection of the dead . . . And if Christ has not been raised, our preaching is useless and so is your faith . . . we are then found to be false witnesses about God that he raised Christ from the dead . . . And if Christ has not been raised, your faith is futile; you are still in your sins" (15:12-17). Such logic almost demands faith. Faith does not make sense without the resurrection of Jesus, not the faith of the early disciples, and not the faith of anyone else. It seems very logical to Paul: "For since death came through a man [Adam], the resurrection of the dead comes also through a man [Jesus]" (15:21). The event of Jesus' resurrection and the expectation of future resurrection are reasonable: "As in Adam all die, so in Christ all will be made alive . . . each in his own turn: Christ, the firstfruits; then, when he comes, those who belong to him" (15:22-23).

Without the resurrection of Jesus, any resurrection seems unreasonable. But resurrection is not unreasonable, because Jesus rose from the dead. Faith is useless apart from the resurrection of Jesus. Since Jesus did rise from the dead, faith makes a lot of sense.

For Paul, the resurrection of Jesus is a very sure fact of human history, one that drives hope for life after death. There is no question of possibly or maybe or of some kind of mis-interpretation or re-interpretation of the resurrection of Jesus. He rose, we believe, and we shall rise too. As many have indicated in a variety of contexts, the growth of Christianity in the early period makes little or no sense unless Jesus did in fact rise from the dead. That is, in effect, what Paul is saying, that if Jesus did not rise from the dead, then his [Paul's] faith and the faith of other Christians in his own day doesn't make a lot of sense. But faith does make a lot of sense, because Jesus did rise from the dead.

## Wanting More Demonstrations of Power

A third way that the New Testament speaks to the questioning of power or miracles comes in the response to requests for more miracles or signs or demonstrations of power. The power of God, especially demonstrated in miracles, is not something that can be turned on or off at anyone's whim, whatever the merits of such a whim might be. Each of the Gospels deals with this particular aspect of the power problem.

Mark and Matthew note the reaction of Jesus to the request for miracles or signs following the feeding of the four thousand. According to Mark 8:11, the Pharisees tested Jesus by asking Him for "a sign from heaven." In His reply, Jesus said, "Why does this generation ask for a miraculous sign? I tell you the truth, no sign will be given to it" (11:12). Matthew's account (Matthew 16:1-4) is similar, although the testing came from both the Pharisees and Sadducees. Jesus replied accordingly, "You know how to interpret the appearance of the sky, but you cannot interpret the signs of the times. A wicked and adulterous generation looks for a miraculous sign, but none will be given it except the sign of Jonah." Luke's account (Luke 11:29-32) does not mention the feeding of the four thousand or the particular Jewish parties. Jesus addressed the "crowds" and said, "This is a wicked generation. It asks for a miraculous sign, but none will be given it except the sign of Jonah. For as Jonah was a sign to the Ninevites, so also will the Son of Man be to this generation."

We have previously observed that John 6 includes John's account of the feeding of the five thousand as well as Jesus' interaction with His disciples and the crowd that followed Him. Jesus said in John 6:26, "I tell you the truth, you are looking for me, not because you saw miraculous signs but because you ate the loaves and had your fill." Consequently, in 6:30, "they" or "the crowd" asked Him, "What miraculous sign then will you give that we may see it and believe you? What will you do?" There would be no sign like they wanted, because Jesus was the sign, as 6:36 says, "But as I told you, you have seen me and still you do not believe."

Previously in John's Gospel the same issue is addressed. In John 2, after the cleansing of the temple (2:13-17), the Jews demanded of Jesus in 2:18, "What miraculous sign can you show us to prove your authority to do all this?" Jesus' answer was not what they expected: "Destroy this temple, and I will raise it again in three days" (2:19). They did not understand that Jesus was speaking of the resurrection of His body, as 2:21 says: "But the temple he had spoken of was his body." Full understanding was to come later as 2:22 explains: "After he was raised from the dead, his disciples recalled what he had said. Then they believed the Scripture and the words that Jesus had spoken."

This rather constant struggle about signs and authority continues to this day. There is no way to completely resolve the difficulty for those who turn a deaf ear or a blind eye to the authority to which the miracles or signs point. Jesus said in John 5:36, in response to the significance of John the Baptist, "For the very work that the Father has given me to finish, and which I am doing, testifies that the Father has sent me. And the Father who sent me has himself testified concerning me. You have never heard his voice nor seen his form, nor does his word dwell in you, for you do not believe the one he sent." The fact is that they did not believe the testimony of John the Baptist or of Jesus, and the testimony of Jesus was reinforced by the miracles or signs. These demonstrations of power are crucial. So John 5:39-40 asserts, "You diligently study the Scriptures because you think that by them you possess eternal life. These are the Scriptures that testify about me, yet you refuse to come to me to have life."

Thus Jesus performed miracles that were signs, but He did them as He wanted them done and not necessarily as others wanted them done. That they worked for some people is obvious since some people, notably His disciples, believed in Him.

## The Nature of Faith

A fourth way in which the New Testament responds to those who question demonstrations of power comes in regard to faith itself. John 10-11 is perhaps most instructive for this purpose. According to 10:24, some Jews asked Jesus, "How long will you keep us in suspense? If you are the Christ, tell us plainly." The response of Jesus was, "I did tell you, but you do not believe. The miracles [Greek *erga*, often translated as "works"] I do in my Father's name speak for me, but you do not believe because you are not my sheep" (10:25-26). Here Jesus expected His works or miracles to speak for Him, to be a testimony to His messianic/Christ nature. But in this case the miracles did not have their desired result. Instead, as 10:31 says, "The Jews picked up stones to stone him." When Jesus asked them which of His works or miracles was leading them to stone Him, they replied that it was not for any particular work or miracle that they were going to stone Him, "but for blasphemy, because you, a mere man, claim to be God" (10:33). This conversation led eventually to the words of 10:37-38 which we have referred to previously: "Do not believe me unless I do what my Father does. But if I do it, even though you do not believe me, believe the miracles [Greek *erga*], that you may know and understand that the Father is in me, and I in the Father."

Subsequently, John 10 says that Jesus went to the place along the Jordan River where John the Baptist had done his baptizing. There were many people who followed Jesus there, and they said, "Though John never performed a miraculous sign, all that John said about this man [Jesus] was true." As a result, "in that place many believed in Jesus" (10:41-42). It did not take miracles or signs to bring everyone to faith. In this case the testimony of John the Baptist was sufficient.

Miracles are not necessary in order for faith to occur. However miracles do point to something or serve as signs of something that must be believed. Miracles and faith go together. You can have one without the other, i.e., can have faith without miracles, but it takes faith to understand the purpose or object of miracles. Without faith there is no progression beyond a mere act or event. Without faith, there is no sign that points to the authority of Jesus.

The account of Lazarus in John 11 continues to show how faith and miracles go together, but not to the point of faith depending on miracles. When Jesus approached the house of the deceased Lazarus, Martha displayed faith without the evidence of the miraculous. She said to Jesus, in 11:21-22, "Lord ... if you had been here, my brother would not have died. But I know that even now God will give you whatever you ask." As their conversation continued in regard to the prospect for the raising of Lazarus and a "last day" resurrection, Jesus sought acknowledgment of His authority: "I am the resurrection and the life. He who believes in me will live, even though he dies; and whoever lives and believes in me will never die. Do you believe this?" (11:25-26). Martha's reply was one of faith in the authority of Jesus: "Yes, Lord ... I believe that you are the Christ, the Son of God, who was to come into the world" (11:27). Subsequently, Mary also demonstrated faith in the authority and *power* of Jesus since she also said, "Lord, if you had been here my brother would not have died" (11:32). But others were of the same conviction since according to 11:37, some of the Jews said, "Could not he who opened the eyes of the blind man have kept this man from dying?"

The faith of Martha, Mary and at least some of the Jews was eventually rewarded. Jesus said in 11:40, "Did I not tell you that if you believed, you would see the glory of God?" Their faith was to be rewarded by evidence of the divine/heavenly authority of Jesus, that evidence being provided by the sign or miracle (a demonstration of power) of the raising of Lazarus in response to the direction of Jesus that the stone should be removed from the tomb of Lazarus. So it was that Jesus prayed to God, "Father, I thank you that you have heard me. I knew that you always hear me, but I said this for the benefit of the people standing here, that they may believe that you sent me" (11:41-42). The faith of the people was to be rewarded by evidence or a demonstration of power which would enhance or insure that faith. The ultimate effect was to cause rebellion in the Jewish leadership. The leaders admitted in 11:47-48, "Here is this man performing many miraculous signs. If we let him go on like this, everyone will believe in him...."

While John 10-11 is not the end of the matter, it does show that faith is not static or fully accomplished at any one point. Faith may precede evidence or power, but faith also follows evidence or power. Thus,

Faith → Authority → Power/Miracle → Faith

but also,

Power/Miracle → Authority → Faith

and,

Power/Miracle → Faith → Authority

and,

Faith → Power/Miracle → Authority → Faith.

Faith is always part of the power-authority relationship. That is simply the norm of the biblical revelation.

## More on Faith with Respect to Power and Authority

Elsewhere the importance of faith in regard to the working of miracles or demonstrations of power is seen in a number of passages. Mark 9:14-32 (see also Matthew 17:14-23 and Luke 9:37-45) contains the account of the healing of a boy with an evil or convulsive spirit. In response to the inability of the disciples to heal the boy, Jesus said in 9:19, "O unbelieving generation, how long shall I stay with you? How long shall I put up with you?" After assessing the boy's condition, Jesus said in 9:23, "Everything is possible for him who believes," to which the boy's father responded in 9:24, "I do believe; help me overcome my unbelief!" In Mathew's account (17:19-21), the disciples, perplexed by their inability to bring healing to the boy, asked Jesus for an explanation of their failure, and Jesus responded, "Because you have so little faith. I tell you the truth, if you have faith as small as a mustard seed, you can say to this mountain, 'Move from here to there' and it will move. Nothing will be impossible for you."

The importance of faith for miracles is also seen in the accounts of Jesus' ministry in His hometown of Nazareth (Mark 6:1-6 and Matthew 13:54-58). Not only did Jesus say that "in his own house . . . a prophet [is] without honor" (Mark 6:4), but 6:5-6 adds, "He could not do any miracles there, except lay his hands on a few sick people and heal them. And he was amazed at their lack of faith." Matthew 13:58 says, "And he did not do many miracles there because of their lack of faith."

The healing of blind Bartimaeus (Mark 10:46-52; Luke 18:35-43) or the blind men (Matthew 20:29-34) at Jericho also shows how closely faith is tied to power. In Mark's account, after Bartimaeus told Jesus that he wanted to see, Jesus said, "Go . . . your faith has healed you" (Mark 10:52), while in Luke 18:42, Jesus said, "Receive your sight; your faith has healed you." By contrast we may note that Jesus' calming of the storm (Mark 4:36-41; Matthew 8:23-27; and Luke 8:22-25) speaks again to the lack of faith. According to Mark 4:40, Jesus' response to the fear of His disciples was, "Why are you so afraid? Do you still have no faith?" According to Luke's account, after Jesus calmed the storm, He asked, "Where is your faith?" Luke adds, "In fear and amazement they asked one another, 'Who is this? He commands even the winds and the water, and they obey him.'"

So it is that faith is inextricably wound up in any consideration of power and authority so far as the New Testament is concerned. It just cannot be any other way. There is no absolute faith-less way in which one can prove that miracles occurred or in which one can authenticate the authority of Jesus by miraculous power. It takes faith, and when anyone, be it scholar or peasant, refuses to exercise faith in the context of miracles or power, there will be no progression to an understanding and acceptance of divine authority.

# Chapter 14

# Conclusion

At the beginning of this study we made the assertion that the themes of authority and power are closely related in the biblical revelation. The weight of the biblical record that we have examined justifies such an assertion. This relationship seems to be more than coincidental. Indeed, the relationship is purposeful, just as Jesus stated in the healing of the paralyzed man according to Mark 2. Power is displayed in order that authority might be confirmed. In the case of the paralyzed man, the power that Jesus displayed in healing the paralytic was for the purpose of confirming Jesus' authority to forgive the sins of the man. To some degree all power exercised in the name of God substantiates the authority of God. Demonstrations of power in the biblical accounts have the purpose of affirming divine authority.

The Bible furnishes an almost inexhaustible record of the relationship between authority and power. This is true in both the Old and New Testaments. This record is of two basic types, that which involves human witnesses and interaction, and that which involves primarily what might be called natural revelation. According to the biblical record, people experience the power of God in a variety of ways, but especially through miracles, and this power demonstrates or affirms the authority of God which often confronts people personally. The power of God is also revealed in the wonders of nature, especially those wonders that involve creation or acts of creation, and this creative power likewise demonstrates or evidences the authority of God.

1 Peter 1:3-9 speaks of faith and hope that endure suffering in anticipation of the return or ultimate revelation of Jesus Christ. 1:8-9 says, "Though you have not seen him, you love him; and even though you do not see him now, you believe in him and . . . are receiving the goal of your faith, the salvation of your souls." Such enduring faith needs support, and it finds sup-

port in exactly the same way that Scripture offers it again and again: first, in dependence upon the power of God manifested in the ministry of God's biblical servants and declared by those servants; and second, in the wondrous power evidenced in nature itself and which the biblical writers regarded as testimony to God's authority. Peter uses the second person in this passage to speak of "you" who "have not seen him," and "do not see him now." But these people who have not seen Jesus nonetheless do indeed "love him," "believe in him," and are "filled with an inexpressible and glorious joy" in anticipation of "the salvation of your souls."

Why do such people believe even though they have not seen? It is because they rely on and trust the testimony of those who have seen. So Peter has had convincing proof, powerful proof of the Lord's authority, in the miracles he has witnessed according to the record of the Gospels, and according to Acts 2:32 where he asserts "we are all witnesses" of the fact of the resurrected Jesus. In 2 Peter 1:12-21, however, Peter also personally insists on the evidence of his own witness of the power of God, such power demonstrated especially in the transfiguration. He says, "We were eyewitnesses," "We ourselves heard," and "We were with him."

So Peter has seen, while those he writes to have not seen. Yet he calls on those who have not seen to endure trials, and commends them for their faith. Since he has seen or witnessed the power of God in Jesus, he knows that the faith of those who have not seen is not misplaced or in vain. It is the same way for us, long removed from the biblical period. We believe without seeing or having seen, because we say "Yes" to the record of those, like Peter, who said they did see. We believe that the power of God was demonstrated in a variety of ways to His biblical servants, and we resign ourselves to the authority of God as declared by those servants.

---

[1] John Piper, *What Jesus Demands from the World* (Wheaton, Illinois: Crossway Books, 2006) 32.
[2] Piper 34.
[3] Piper 35.
[4] John Marsh, "Authority" in *The Interpreter's Dictionary of the Bible*, Vol. A-D, New York: Abingdon Press, 1962.
[5] Edward Laarman, "Power; Might" in *The International Standard Bible Encyclopedia*, Vol. 3: K-P, Grand Rapids: Eerdmans Publishing Co., 1986.
[6] See *Hume on Human Nature and the Understanding*, ed. Antony Flew, New York: Collier Books, 1962, especially Section 10, "Of Miracles," 115-136.
[7] Ernest Renan, *The Life of Jesus*, New York: The Modern Library, 1927, "Author's Introduction," 25-65, especially 58-61.
[8] Albert Schweitzer, *The Quest of the Historical Jesus*, ed. John Bowden, Minneapolis: Fortress Press, 2001.

[9] Schweitzer 14-26.
[10] Schweitzer 29-31.
[11] Schweitzer 47-55.
[12] Schweitzer 74-90.
[13] Schweitzer 124-142.
[14] Rudolf Bultmann, et. al., *Kerygma and Myth*, New York: Harper and Brothers, 1961.
[15] Bultmann 4.
[16] Bultmann 4-5.
[17] Bultmann 8.
[18] Bultmann 34.
[19] Bultmann 39.
[20] Bultmann 42.
[21] C. S. Lewis, *Miracles*, New York: The Macmillan Company, 1947.
[22] Lewis 17.
[23] Lewis 31.
[24] Lewis 32.
[25] Lewis 48-49.
[26] Lewis 49.
[27] Lewis 59.
[28] Lewis 61.
[29] Lewis 62-63.
[30] Lewis 170.
[31] Lewis 171.

www.ingramcontent.com/pod-product-compliance
Lightning Source LLC
Chambersburg PA
CBHW021812220426
43662CB00006B/287